W9-BFF-041

so JANE

Crafts and Recipes for an Austen-Inspired Life

Hollie Keith
Recipes by Jennifer Adams
Photography by Susan Barnson Hayward

GIBBS SMITH
TO ENRICH AND INSPIRE HUMANKIND

CONTENTS

INTRODUCTION

We can never get enough Jane Austen. We read and reread her novels, watch the movies, and even go see every new movie Colin Firth appears in just to get a glimpse of the former Mr. Darcy. We buy journals and calendars, quote books and magnets and cards. We buy them for ourselves and our fellow Austen lovers. "I Heart Jane!" our T-Shirts and throw pillows proclaim.

Just what Jane Austen means to us and why her work has endured so splendidly for two centuries is a subject for another book—and, in fact, many well-written books, scholarly and otherwise, are devoted to just that question. (*A Jane Austen Education: How Six Novels Taught Me about Love, Friendship, and the Things That Really Matter*, by William Deresiewicz, is not to be missed.)

Yet this book attempts to do something altogether different. In honor of Jane Austen's 200th birthday we present to you *So Jane*. It brings all things Austen into your daily life of decorating, gift giving, and entertaining. It's a collection of Austen-inspired crafts and recipes that weave together story lines and characters from Austen's six novels, with a glimpse into Austen's world and daily life as well.

The book is organized by chapter, one for each novel. Use the menus and themed crafts for parties and get-togethers or just to have fun on a rainy afternoon. *So Jane* also includes great crafts to do with kids. In these pages you'll find inspiration for a Jane Austen–themed bridal shower, a tea with friends, or a birthday party for your favorite Janeite.

Enjoy your own Box Hill Picnic or throw a Christmas dinner party with the menu from the Netherfield Ball chapter. Decorate with Emma and Mr. Knightley's Paper Chandelier, make tea towels and handmade soap for guests who are staying over, or create wind chimes as gifts for friends.

"All Jane Austen, all the time!" Bernadette exclaims in the movie *The Jane Austen Book Club*. This book will help you achieve just that. And there are worse mottos, we think.

What Would Jane Do? Get cooking and crafting!

Breakfast in Bath

MENU

Spiced Hot Cocoa

Clotted Cream

Soft-Boiled Eggs

Scones

Raspberry Jam

Apple Pastries

CRAFTS

Janeite Decoupage Letters

Jane Silhouette Placemats

Decorative Egg Cozies

Doily Clay Ornaments

Patchwork Fabric Bowl

CHAPTER 1

Northanger Abbey

"Happy, happy breakfast!"
—*Northanger Abbey*

JANEITE
Decoupage
LETTERS

What better way to start things off than by making decoupage letters that spell the word "Janeite," declaring to all who visit your home what literary star is your favorite. These letters would also make an excellent table display for any Jane Austen–themed party.

Materials

5-inch cardboard letters in J, A, N, E, I, T, E (from Jo-Ann Fabric and Craft Stores)

Variety of patterned and colored papers (thicker works better)

Craft knife or scissors

Mod Podge, in matte

Medium-sized plastic bowl

Sponge brush

Walnut ink in spray bottle

Tissues

Instructions

STEP 1: Assign each letter a paper pattern. Find a combination that looks good.

STEP 2: Starting with the J, place it face down on the back of its corresponding paper. Using the cardboard letter as a template, trace its shape onto the paper with a pencil. Cut out the letter shape.

STEP 3: Pour some Mod Podge in a plastic bowl.

STEP 4: Use a sponge brush to apply Mod Podge to the front and back of the paper letter cutout, making sure the sealer is covering all areas. Stick the cutout on the front of the J and press down to adhere.

STEP 5: Repeat steps 2 and 4 for the remaining letters. Let sealer dry overnight.

STEP 6: Working with one letter at a time, spray walnut ink on the outside edges. Use tissues to blend and work in the ink for a distressed and antique effect. Let ink dry overnight.

TIP: If using as a table display, cover both sides of each letter for a complete, finished look.

SPICED
Hot Cocoa

8 ounces dark chocolate
4 cups whole milk
1 cinnamon stick
1 teaspoon vanilla extract
3 teaspoons sugar
$\frac{1}{8}$ teaspoon salt
Whipped cream, optional

Finely chop the chocolate into small pieces.

Place the milk in a small, heavy pan and bring to a simmer over low heat,
being careful not to scald it.

Add the cinnamon stick and remove pan from heat. Allow the cinnamon to
steep for 10 minutes. Remove the cinnamon stick and discard.

Return pan to heat. Stir in the vanilla, sugar, salt, and chocolate pieces;
whisk until chocolate has melted. Once the chocolate has melted,
heat for 4 minutes, stirring constantly.

Serve with a dollop of whipped cream, if desired.

Makes 4 servings

Hot cocoa reached the British Isles as a drink as early as the 1650s. It made
its way from Spain, where chiles were a major ingredient in chocolate drinks.
This recipe for hot chocolate is perhaps less historically
accurate, but better for modern tastes.

> This Jane Silhouette Placemat design is a "novel" idea for the breakfast table. Follow the supply list and instructions here to make one placemat. Make more placemats in complementary fabrics and felts to create a collectible series by embroidering each of Austen's novel titles on a placemat.

JANE
Silhouette
PLACEMATS

Materials

Fusible interfacing

Iron

2 (17 x 17-inch) pieces coordinating fabric (small-patterned fabric will work better than large-patterned)

Jane Austen Silhouette template (see page 138)

Scissors

1 (9 x 12-inch) sheet felt in black

Dressmaker pins

2 embroidery needles

Embroidery thread in black and 2 contrasting colors

Austen Novel Title templates (see page 138)

Sewing machine

Instructions

STEP 1: Cut interfacing to the size of the fabric. Iron the interfacing to the back side of the fabric to be used on the front of the placemat.

STEP 2: Use the Jane Austen Silhouette template to cut a silhouette shape from the piece of felt. Pin to the front fabric.

STEP 3: Using an embroidery needle and black thread, sew the silhouette to the placemat with a running stitch. Secure thread with a knot on the back.

STEP 4: Choose an Austen book title to embroider on the front of the placemat. Copy the template from page 138, cut it out, and pin it to the front of the fabric.

STEP 5: Using the 2 contrasting threads, embroider the font outline with a couching stitch. Thread both needles, one with a base thread (pink thread in photo) and the other with contrasting thread (white thread in photo). Pull both through to front. Hold the base thread in place with your fingers as you move along the font lines. Use the needle with

contrasting thread to sew "stripes" over the top of the base thread. Tie off both threads on back with knots.

STEP 6: Lay front and back pieces of placemat fabric together, right sides facing each other. Secure with pins.

STEP 7: Sew around edges, with a $\frac{1}{2}$-inch seam allowance. Leave a 5-inch opening so you can turn the fabric right side out once finished. Clip the corners of fabric to avoid bunching when turned right side out. Make sure not to cut into the seam.

STEP 8: Turn fabric right side out. Sew the opening closed with a blind stitch. Press placemat with a warm iron.

TIP: For an Austen-themed gathering, use the Jane Austen Silhouette template to decorate garlands, coasters, tablecloths and fabric napkins.

CLOTTED *Cream*

1 cup heavy cream
$\frac{1}{3}$ cup sour cream
1 tablespoon powdered
   sugar

Place heavy cream in a medium bowl and whip with an electric mixer until stiff peaks form. Whisk in the sour cream and powdered sugar by hand until just combined. Keep refrigerated.

Makes 8 servings

Clotted Cream, sometimes called Devonshire Cream, is delicious served on scones with strawberry or raspberry jam and a pot of tea.

SOFT_BOILED
Eggs

6 large eggs
Salt and pepper,
to taste

Place eggs in a saucepan large
enough to keep them in a single
layer. Fill the pan with cold water,
covering eggs by an inch.

Place over medium-high heat and
bring water to a boil. Turn off heat,
cover, and let stand 1$\frac{1}{2}$–2 minutes.
Remove eggs from water. Serve
immediately in egg cups.

Crack the tops and eat the eggs out
of the shell, sprinkling with salt
and pepper.

Makes 6 servings

Served in pretty egg cups with Decorative Egg Cozies (see page 17),
these make a fancy addition to a morning breakfast or brunch.

DECORATIVE
Egg COZIES

Whether you're right on time for a high-society breakfast or fashionably late, these fun egg cozies will keep your Soft-Boiled Eggs (see page 15) warm until your arrival. This list of supplies will make 4 cozies.

Materials

Egg cozy template (see page 139)

Scissors

8 (5 x 5-inch) pieces felt in coordinating colors

Fabric scraps with designs for appliqué and sewing

Thread in coordinating colors

12 inches lace ribbon

Dressmaker pins

Sewing machine with embroidery foot

Instructions

STEP 1: Use the egg cozy template to cut 8 pieces of felt (4 matching color pairs).

STEP 2: Cut out designs from fabric scraps and pin to one of the felt pieces. Use a sewing machine fitted with an embroidery foot to sew around the inside edges of the appliqués (edges are left raw). Don't worry about the stitches looking messy. Any unevenness adds to the handmade charm.

STEP 3: For each cozy, take a matching pair of felt pieces and pin their right sides together.

STEP 4: Cut 3 inches of ribbon for each cozy.

STEP 5: Fold ribbon in half and insert folded edge in the top of each cozy, with $1/2$ inch of each ribbon end sticking out of the edge on the wrong side of the fabric (folded edge will be "sandwiched" inside the felt pieces).

STEP 6: Using your sewing machine, sew around the edge of each cozy, about $1/4$ inch from edge, leaving the bottom edge open.

STEP 7: Cut notches along the rounded edge of each cozy, making sure not to cut into the seam.

STEP 8: Turn each cozy right side out.

DOILY *Clay* ORNAMENTS

A set of these sparkling delicate beauties would be a nice decoration at any high-society gathering in Bath, or most definitely in your home. These are lovely hanging on a potted miniature tree or on bare branches gathered in a vase. Another idea is to decorate a party table by placing several all around the top of the table. If they're used this way, there's no need to poke a hole in the clay for hanging.

Materials

1 (16-ounce) package paperclay, in white

Rolling pin

Cutting board

Crocheted doilies in a variety of sizes (found at most craft stores)

Craft knife

Toothpick

Paintbrush

Acrylic paints in variety of colors (ornaments shown have a pearl finish)

Glitter, fine

Instructions

STEP 1: Soften the paperclay by kneading it a little.

STEP 2: Use a rolling pin to roll out the clay on top of a cutting board. Roll to ¼-inch thickness.

STEP 3: Place a crocheted doily on top of the paperclay and gently press the design of the doily into the clay in all areas.

STEP 4: Carefully cut around the edges of the doily with a craft knife, and remove the extra clay.

STEP 5: Remove the crocheted doily from the top of the ornament. Smooth any rough edges with a toothpick and your fingers.

STEP 6: If planning to hang the ornament, use a toothpick to poke a hole in the top, about ¼ inch from the edge. Let the ornament dry and harden for at least 2 hours.

STEP 7: Apply a coat of acrylic paint to the top of the ornament. Let dry. Apply a second coat and then sprinkle glitter over the top. Once dry, turn the ornament over and paint the back.

PATCHWORK *Fabric* BOWL

Materials

1 (12-inch-diameter, 3½-inch-deep) bowl to use as a guide

32 or more (3 x 3-inch) squares of wool fabric cut using pinking shears to prevent fraying (32 squares are used in the bowl shown in photo)

Sponge brush

Mod Podge, matte

Put this colorful bowl to work holding the Scones from page 22. Make sure to line the inside of the bowl with a tea towel, which will protect the finish on the inside of the bowl as well as keep the scones warm.

Instructions

STEP 1: Wrap guide bowl with a plastic bag. Lay bowl face down on work area (see photo below).

STEP 2: Apply Mod Podge to each side of a fabric square and then lay it on the top of the inverted guide bowl, as shown. Building from the middle and working in rows, add the fabric squares that have been prepared with Mod Podge, creating a patchwork effect. Let dry overnight

or until completely dry. Regularly check the bowl to make sure Mod Podge is not adhering to the plastic bag.

STEP 3: Once dry, remove the patchwork bowl from the guide bowl. Place patchwork bowl inside the guide bowl and add another coat of sealer to the inside of the patchwork bowl. Let dry.

STEP 4: Apply one more coat of Mod Podge to the inside and outside of the fabric bowl, allowing time to dry in between coats. Note: Mod Podge isn't food-safe, so use a tea towel or other protective liner when filling the bowl with scones or other baked goods.

TIP: Use scissors to trim around the edge of the finished bowl.

SCONES

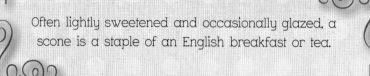

Often lightly sweetened and occasionally glazed, a
scone is a staple of an English breakfast or tea.

2 cups flour
¼ cup sugar
2 teaspoons baking powder
¼ teaspoon salt
⅓ cup cold unsalted butter
1 egg, lightly beaten
1 teaspoon vanilla or almond extract
½ cup heavy cream, plus more for brushing

Preheat oven to 350 degrees F.

Sift dry ingredients together in a medium bowl. Cut in butter until
mixture resembles coarse crumbs. Make a well in the center and
add the egg, vanilla, and cream. Mix together until just combined.
Do not over mix.

Place a piece of waxed paper on a work surface and flour lightly.

With a floured rolling pin, roll out the dough to ½-inch thickness.

Cut out scones with a floured cutter. Brush the tops with cream and
bake for 9–12 minutes, or until golden brown.

Makes 12 scones

RASPBERRY

Jam

1 (1^5/$_8$-ounce) envelope freezer jam pectin
1^1/$_2$ cups sugar
4 cups crushed raspberries

Combine freezer jam pectin and sugar in a large bowl;
stir until blended. Add crushed raspberries and stir to combine.
Continue stirring mixture for 3 minutes.

Pour jam into clean jars or freezer containers.
Let stand until thickened, about 30 minutes.
Serve immediately and refrigerate up to
three weeks or freeze up to one year.

Makes 4 cups

Jellies in Austen's time were not like jams but molded gelatins. However, jams,
marmalades, and such were also made and served. Here is a recipe for
raspberry jam that works well served on scones along with clotted cream.

APPLE
Pastries

2 tablespoons lemon juice
4 cups water
4 Granny Smith apples, peeled, cored and diced
2 tablespoons butter
1 cup brown sugar
1 teaspoon ground cinnamon
2 tablespoons cornstarch
2 tablespoons water
1 (17.25-ounce) package frozen puff pastry sheets, thawed

GLAZE
1 cup powdered sugar
1–2 tablespoons milk or more as needed
1 teaspoon vanilla extract

"When you receive this, our guests will be all gone or going; and I shall be left to the comfortable disposal of my time, to ease of mind from the torments of rice puddings and apple dumplings."
—Letter from Jane Austen to her sister Cassandra, January 7, 1807

Preheat oven to 400 degrees F.

Combine the lemon juice and water in a large bowl. Place the diced apples in the water to keep them from turning brown.

Melt butter in a large saute pan over medium heat. Remove apples from water and place them into the hot pan. Cook and stir for about 2 minutes until apples soften. Add brown sugar and cinnamon. Continue to cook and stir for 2 more minutes.

In a small bowl, stir together cornstarch and water. Add to the apples and mix well. Continue to cook and stir for 1 more minute, or until sauce has thickened. Remove from heat and cool slightly.

Unfold pastry sheets and trim each one into a square. Cut each square into 4 smaller squares. Spoon cooked apples onto the centers of each square and fold into a triangle shape, pressing edges together to seal. Do not over-fill.

Place filled pastries on a baking sheet that has been sprayed with nonstick cooking spray and bake for 25 minutes, or until pastries are puffed and lightly browned. Cool completely before glazing.

In a small bowl, mix together the powdered sugar, milk, and vanilla. Add more milk as necessary to reach desired consistency. Drizzle glaze over cooled pastries.

Makes 8

CHAPTER 2

Sense and Sensibility

"You MUST drink tea with us to night."
—Sense and Sensibility

Tea with the Middletons

MENU

Crumpets

Orange Custard

Queen Cakes

Rose Petal Tea

Lemon Drizzle Cake

CRAFTS

Tea Towel For Guests

Hand-Poured Sensible Soap

Margaret's Vintage Fabric Garland

Honey-Lemon Teaspoons

Tea Time Table Runner

TEA
Towel
FOR
GUESTS

Guests to your home will be delighted to see a teapot or tea time pastries kept warm by this charming tea towel. The apple and pear appliqués are dotted with a popular Regency-era shade, pomona green, or apple green as it's widely called today. The flower appliqués are repurposed from vintage handkerchiefs.

Materials

1 yard white cotton twill fabric

Dressmaker pins

Sewing machine, running foot and embroidery foot

1 spool white thread

1 fat quarter patterned fabric

Regular fabric scissors and pinking shears

6 fat quarters in coordinating fabrics to be used for the pear and apple. The finished pear shape is 7 X $4^{1}/_{2}$ inches. The finished apple shape is $3^{1}/_{2}$ x $4^{1}/_{2}$ inches.

Pear and apple patterns (see page 139)

Brown felt for the stems and fruit seeds

1 spool brown thread

Printed flowers clipped from vintage handkerchiefs or other fabrics

Instructions

FOR THE BASE

 STEP 1: Cut cotton twill fabric to 23 x 17 inches.

 STEP 2: Fold over edges of fabric $^{1}/_{4}$ inch. Secure with pins.

 STEP 3: Use sewing machine fitted with a running foot to sew a running stitch around all edges using the white thread.

 STEP 4: Cut fat quarter patterned fabric to $21^{1}/_{2}$ x 15 inches. Trim edges $^{1}/_{4}$ inch with pinking shears. Finished size should be 21 x $14^{1}/_{2}$ inches.

 STEP 5: Sew patterned fabric to twill fabric with a zigzag stitch $^{1}/_{4}$ inch from edge.

FOR THE PEAR APPLIQUÉ

 STEP 1: Choose 3 coordinating fabrics for the pear appliqué. Use pear patterns to cut shapes. Use leftover handkerchief fabric (or solid-colored fabric) to serve as the base for the pear. Cut out a stem shape and 4 seed shapes from the brown felt.

 STEP 2: Organize pear shapes on top of towel base and pin in place.

FOR THE APPLE APPLIQUÉ

 STEP 1: Choose 3 coordinating fabrics for the apple appliqué. Use apple patterns to cut shapes. Use leftover handkerchief fabric (or solid-colored fabric) to serve as the base for the apple. Cut out a stem shape and 3 seed shapes from the brown felt.

 STEP 2: Organize apple shapes on top of towel base and pin in place.

FOR THE PRINTED FLOWERS

 STEP 1: Carefully cut 3–5 printed flowers from vintage handkerchiefs or other fabric.

 STEP 2: Organize flowers on top of towel base and pin in place.

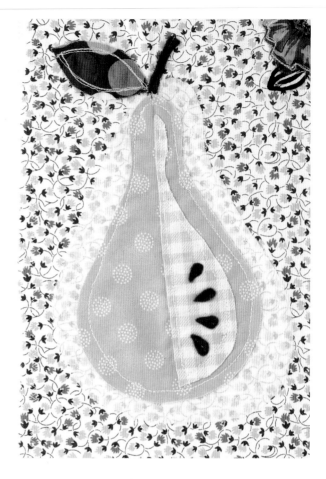

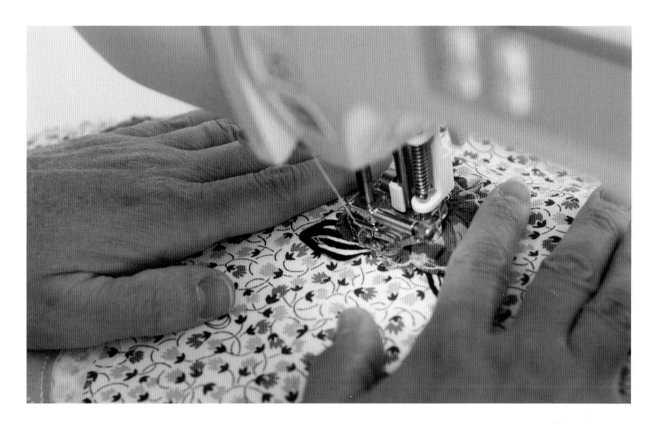

PUT IT TOGETHER

 STEP 1: Use a sewing machine fitted with an embroidery foot to sew around the inside edges of the flower cutouts and fruit shapes (except for the stems and seeds). Don't worry about the stitches looking messy. Any unevenness adds to the handmade charm.

 STEP 2: Switch thread color to brown and replace embroidery foot with a running foot on the sewing machine. Sew stems and seeds to the fruit.

 STEP 3: To extend the life of the tea towel, wash in cold water on gentle cycle and hang to dry.

CRUMPETS

2 cups plus 2 tablespoons flour
2 teaspoons instant yeast
1 teaspoon sugar
$\frac{1}{2}$ teaspoon salt
$1\frac{1}{4}$ cups warm water
$1\frac{1}{4}$ cups warm milk
1 teaspoon vanilla extract
4 (3-inch) crumpet molds or metal cookie cutters

Whisk flour, yeast, sugar, and salt together in a large mixing bowl. Combine water, milk, and vanilla in a separate bowl. Quickly whisk the milk mixture into the dry ingredients until batter is thick and smooth. Cover with a towel and let rise in a warm place until spongy, about 1 hour. Stir to reduce sponginess.

Preheat oven to 150 degrees F.

Spray a large saute pan and crumpet molds with nonstick cooking spray. Heat pan over medium-low heat. Place molds into the frying pan and let them heat up. Spoon batter into the molds, filling them about halfway. Let the crumpets cook until the bottoms are browned and the tops appear almost dry and have popped bubbles, about 5 minutes.

Remove crumpets in molds from pan using tongs and then remove molds from the crumpets. Flip and return crumpets to the frying pan to brown the other side, about 1–2 minutes. Repeat with remaining dough. Keep cooked crumpets warm on a rack in preheated oven until ready to serve.

Makes 12 crumpets

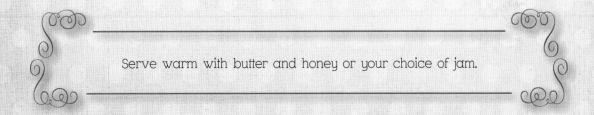

Serve warm with butter and honey or your choice of jam.

These rose-shaped soaps are a perfect accoutrement to a guest bathroom. Unlike traditional Regency soaps, these are free of lye and wood ashes. Rather, a few drops of English Rose fragrance and a simple spritz of rubbing alcohol is all that's needed for utmost cleanliness.

HAND-POURED *Sensible* SOAP

Materials

1 block (about 16 ounces) clear melt-and-pour glycerin soap base (Bramble Berry)

Liquid pink food coloring (do not use gel)

1 teaspoon English Rose fragrance oil (Bramble Berry)

Plastic rose mold (see Note)

Spray bottle filled with rubbing alcohol

Instructions

 STEP 1: Heat glycerin in the microwave according to package directions.

 STEP 2: Once glycerin is melted, add drops of food coloring until desired color is achieved, and add fragrance oil.

 STEP 3: Spray the inside of the rose mold with rubbing alcohol. Pour glycerin into rose mold. Spray the rose backs with rubbing alcohol.

 STEP 4: When glycerin is hard, turn the mold over on top of a cutting board to release the soaps. You may need to use a small knife around the edges of the soaps to loosen them from the mold.

NOTE: The number of roses you make depends on the size of rose mold used. The roses shown in the photo measure $3\frac{1}{2}$ inches in diameter and were made using a plastic form with 2 molds from Bramble Berry.

ORANGE *Custard*

2 cups half-and-half
4 eggs
$\frac{1}{2}$ teaspoon nutmeg
$\frac{1}{2}$ teaspoon vanilla extract
2 tablespoons orange juice
1 tablespoon orange zest plus more
   for garnish
$\frac{1}{2}$ cup sugar
Whipped cream

Preheat oven to 350 degrees F.

In a medium bowl, combine all ingredients with a whisk until smooth. Place 6 ramekins or custard cups in a large, deep baking dish and divide the mixture among them. Carefully pour hot water into the dish until it reaches halfway up the sides of the cups.

Place the pan in the oven and bake for 30–45 minutes. Custards are done when a knife inserted into the center comes out clean. Do not over bake or custards will crack.

Cool and serve in ramekins topped with whipped cream and orange zest.

Makes 6 servings

Baked custards have been served as desserts for centuries, and the ingredients and instructions have remained much the same. This custard could easily have been served in Jane Austen's time.

QUEEN *Cakes*

½ cup butter, softened
½ cup sugar
Finely grated zest of 1 lemon
2 eggs, beaten
1 cup flour
1 teaspoon baking powder
¼ cup currants, optional
12-cup cupcake pan or 6 ovenproof
   teacups
Powdered sugar for dusting or
   frosting, optional

Recipes for cupcakes appear as early as the 1700s. A "cupcake" was a small cake that was baked in a teacup or ceramic mug. These cakes were called queen cakes in the Regency period. Most of the queen cakes served during this time would have been turned out of the cups once baked, and then iced.

Preheat oven to 350 degrees F. Butter the cups of a 12-cup cupcake pan or 6 ovenproof teacups. If using the teacups, place them on a baking sheet.

In a large mixing bowl, combine the butter and sugar with a hand mixer until creamy. Add the lemon zest and beat until light and fluffy. Add the eggs gradually. Sift the flour together with the baking powder and fold into the batter. Fold in currants if using.

Divide the mixture between the cupcake pan or teacups and bake for 20–30 minutes, until cakes have risen and are golden brown. Watch them carefully and note that the smaller the cake, the more quickly it will bake. Cakes are done when they spring back lightly when touched in the center.

Remove cakes from pan and cool on a wire rack, or leave in teacups to cool. Dust with powdered sugar or add frosting before serving, if desired.

Makes 6–12 cakes

Create a fun tea time backdrop with this fabric garland, which is also versatile décor for a girl's room. A vintage look is achieved with fabric patterns and distressing the edges of the roses by burning them with a candle flame.

MARGARET'S
Vintage
FABRIC GARLAND

Materials

FOR GARLAND FLAGS

9 (5 x 9-inch) pieces felt (any neutral or muted color is fine)

9 (10-inch) pieces burlap, cut from a (6$\frac{1}{2}$-inch x 30-foot) roll burlap garland

18 (5 x 9-inch) pieces patterned fabric (9 matching pairs), cut with pinking shears to avoid fraying

9 (7-inch) pieces decorative lace

3 yards white pom-pom trim

Scissors

Dressmaker pins

Sewing machine

FOR EACH ROSE (YOU WILL BE MAKING 9)

6 circles white acetate fabric cut in the following sizes: 6 inches, 5$\frac{1}{2}$ inches, 5 inches, 4$\frac{1}{2}$ inches, 4 inches, 3 inches

4 (6-inch) circles white tulle

Scissors

Candle

Pearl floral spray

Hot glue gun and glue sticks

Instructions

 STEP 1: Stack each of the 9 garland flags from the bottom layer to the top layer in this order:

- Felt, to use as a backing
- Burlap, with $\frac{1}{2}$-inch overlap at top and bottom
- 1 matching pair patterned fabric pieces
- Decorative lace, placed at bottom of each flag with $\frac{1}{4}$-inch overlap on each side
- Pom-pom trim, placed along the top of flags

 STEP 2: Space flags evenly along the pom-pom trim. Fold down $\frac{1}{2}$-inch overlap at the burlap tops. Secure all layers together with pins.

 STEP 3: Fold ends of decorative lace over flag edges and pin in place.

 STEP 4: Sew all layers of flag tops together using a running stitch. Sew all layers of bottom flags together using a running stitch.

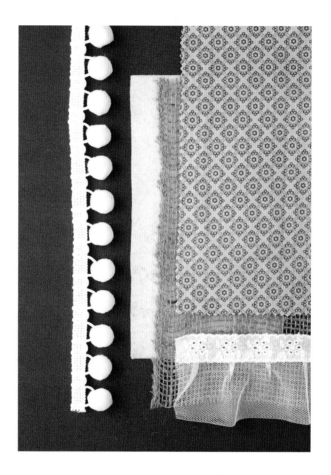

FOR ROSES

 STEP 1: Use the Rose Petal template from (page 140) to cut the petal shapes from the circles of acetate and tulle. Stack all same-size petal pieces together. Stack tulle petals separately from the acetate ones.

 STEP 2: To char the edges of the acetate petals, carefully hold the edges over a candle flame. This will take some time. Working too quickly will result in mistakes with burning the material too much. (Note: Acetate fabric must be used to get the charred look that's shown in the photo.) The heat from the flame will cause the material to curve to a concave shape.

 STEP 3: Once all acetate petals are charred, it's time to build the roses!

Stack petals in this order:

- 6-inch acetate petal
- Tulle petal
- $5\frac{1}{2}$-inch acetate petal
- Tulle petal
- 5-inch acetate petal
- Tulle petal
- $4\frac{1}{2}$-inch acetate petal
- Tulle petal
- 4-inch acetate petal
- 3-inch acetate petal

 STEP 4: Take 5 floral spray stems and fold them in half. Secure together by knotting a piece of thread around the folded end.

 STEP 5: Use the sharp end of the scissors to poke a hole in the middle of the petal stack, being careful not to make the hole too large. Guide the folded end of the floral spray through the hole on the front side of the petal stack.

 STEP 6: Apply hot glue from a glue gun to the folded spray end on the backside of the petal stack. Use enough glue on the back petal so the entire rose can be glued to the front of one of the garland flags.

HONEY–
Lemon
TEASPOONS

Materials

3 tablespoons corn syrup

2 tablespoons water

$\frac{1}{4}$ cup plus 1 tablespoon honey, divided

$\frac{3}{4}$ cup sugar

1 teaspoon lemon juice

14–16 teaspoons, metal or plastic

Silicone-covered parchment

Instructions

 STEP 1: In a medium saucepan with a candy thermometer attached to the side, bring the corn syrup, water, $\frac{1}{4}$ cup honey, and sugar to a boil on medium-high heat. Stir the ingredients with a silicone spatula. Try not to splatter the mixture on the sides of the pan.

 STEP 2: Once the mixture is boiling, let the temperature reach the hard-crack stage, at 300 degrees F. Do not stir. While waiting for the temperature to rise, add the lemon juice—but don't stir it in. The boiling action will take care of it. Once the hard-crack stage has been reached, remove pan from heat, quickly add the additional tablespoon of honey, and stir to combine.

 STEP 3: Lay teaspoons on a sheet of silicone-covered parchment. Use a spoon to drop candy onto the teaspoons. Let candy cool and harden, about 20–30 minutes.

Yields 14–16 teaspoons

Paired with Rose Petal Tea (see facing page), these flavored teaspoons will add the right amount of sweetness and zest to a hot cup, resulting in a tasty blend indeed. If entertaining a group of friends for a tea party, display the teaspoons tableside in a fan style or set them spoon side up in a lovely container.

ROSE *Petal* TEA

4 cups water
2 cups fresh rose petals (edible, organic, and pesticide free)
4 Honey-Lemon Teaspoons (see facing page)

Clip the white bases from the rose petals and discard.
Rinse the petals and pat dry with paper towels.

Place the petals in a small saucepan and cover with
water. Bring to a simmer over medium-high heat.
Simmer for 5 minutes.

Remove from heat and strain
the hot rose petal liquid
into teacups. Serve with
Honey-Lemon Teaspoons.

Makes 4 servings

"Sir John never came
to the Dashwoods
without either inviting
them to dine at the
park the next day, or
to drink tea with them
that evening."
—*Sense and Sensibility*

TEA TIME
Table Runner

Materials

7 (12 x 12-inch) vintage handkerchiefs

Dressmaker pins

Sewing machine

White thread

One must have an attractive back-drop on which to serve tea. This collection of vintage handkerchiefs fashioned into a table runner would make a nice heirloom to be passed down to a future-generation Janeite for her tea parties. You can easily find these in an antiques or second-hand store.

Instructions

STEP 1: Overlap ends of two handkerchiefs. Pin to secure.

STEP 2: Sew a running stitch to attach the two hankies.

STEP 3: Keep pinning and sewing a hanky to the end of the last hanky until all are sewn.

STEP 4: To keep the table runner in its best heirloom form, wash by hand with gentle soap in cool water. Hang to dry. Press with a warm iron.

LEMON DRIZZLE
Cake

1½ cups flour
1 teaspoon baking powder
½ teaspoon salt
1 cup butter, softened

1 cup sugar
4 eggs
1 teaspoon vanilla extract
¼ cup lemon juice

GLAZE
⅓ cup powdered sugar
⅓ cup lemon juice

Preheat oven to 350 degrees F. Butter a 6-cup loaf pan and line with waxed paper.

In a medium bowl, combine dry ingredients. In a separate bowl, combine the butter and sugar with a hand mixer until creamy. Add the eggs, one at a time, mixing well after each addition. Stir in the vanilla.

Add the dry ingredients alternately with the lemon juice to the butter mixture. Mix just until smooth. Pour into prepared pan and bake for 45–50 minutes. Cake is done when a toothpick inserted in the center comes out dry and almost clean.

Prepare the glaze by mixing the powdered sugar with the lemon juice in a non-metallic bowl. When the cake is done, let it cool in the pan 15 minutes. Run a knife around the sides of the pan and turn the cake out onto a rack. Peel off the waxed paper.

Spread the glaze over the top of the cake with a pastry brush and let it drizzle down the sides. Let it soak in. Repeat until all the glaze has been used. Cool and slice cake into pieces. Serve at room temperature.

Makes 12 servings

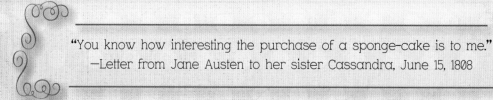

"You know how interesting the purchase of a sponge-cake is to me."
—Letter from Jane Austen to her sister Cassandra, June 15, 1808

Charles Musgrove

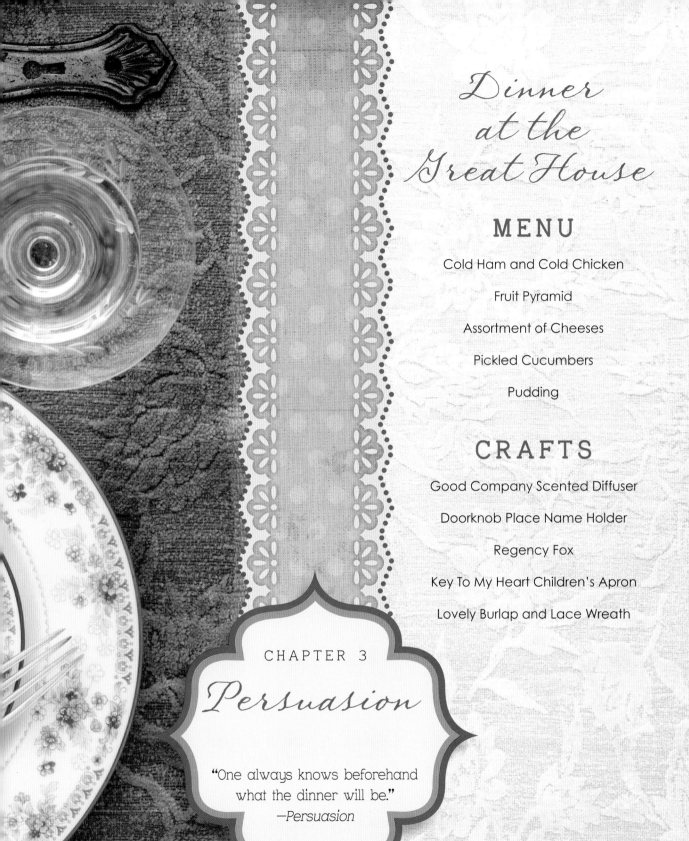

Dinner at the Great House

MENU

Cold Ham and Cold Chicken

Fruit Pyramid

Assortment of Cheeses

Pickled Cucumbers

Pudding

CRAFTS

Good Company Scented Diffuser

Doorknob Place Name Holder

Regency Fox

Key To My Heart Children's Apron

Lovely Burlap and Lace Wreath

CHAPTER 3

Persuasion

"One always knows beforehand
what the dinner will be."
—*Persuasion*

GOOD COMPANY

Scented
DIFFUSER

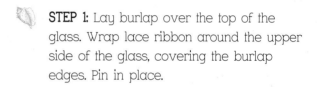

"My idea of good company . . . is the company of clever, well-informed people, who have a great deal of conversation; that is what I call good company." —Anne Elliot, *Persuasion*

Materials

1 glass at least 5 inches deep

Fragrance oil, enough to fill 3 or $3\frac{1}{2}$ inches of the glass

1 (6 x 6-inch) piece burlap (looser weave works better)

1 piece lace ribbon cut to size of glass diameter (add $\frac{1}{2}$ inch for overlap)

Dressmaker pins

Pinking shears

Needle and thread

6–8 diffuser reeds from a craft store

Instructions

STEP 1: Lay burlap over the top of the glass. Wrap lace ribbon around the upper side of the glass, covering the burlap edges. Pin in place.

STEP 2: Hand sew the lace to the burlap (sew while burlap is either on or off the glass, whichever is easier for you).

STEP 3: Remove the lace-burlap cover and fill the glass with fragrance oil. Replace cover.

STEP 4: Insert diffuser reeds through the burlap threads.

TIP: Change fragrance to suit the seasons. For a more authentic fragrance reflective of the Regency era, use oils that smell like rose, lavender, violet or lilac.

Add a touch of antique appeal to the dinner table at your Great House with doorknob place name holders. For an eclectic vintage look, mix and match knobs found at antiques stores and stores that carry vintage-style hardware, such as Anthropologie.

DOORKNOB
Place Name
HOLDER

Materials

1 (6-yard) package 20-gauge wire

Wire cutters

Round bending pliers for wire

Decorative button

Hot glue gun and glue sticks

Antique or antique-style doorknob

Instructions

STEP 1: Cut 8 inches of wire.

STEP 2: Use the pliers to shape one end of the wire into a spiral loop.

STEP 3: Use hot glue to attach a decorative button to the front of the spiral loop. Make sure glue doesn't close up the entire spiral.

STEP 4: Put hot glue in the hole on the backside of the doorknob. Stick the straight end of the wire in the hot glue and hold until the glue sets.

STEP 5: Write a dinner guest's name on a piece of cardstock and slip the bottom edge between the wire loop.

This Regency Fox is a cute gift for a child. Kids can easily help by cutting out the fabric pieces too. The instructions below describe how to make the fox with the lace collar.

REGENCY *Fox*

Materials

- Fox body template (see page 141)
- Fox head template (see page 141)
- Regular fabric scissors and pinking shears
- 1 yard solid-print fabric
- White felt
- Black felt
- Embroidery needle and black embroidery thread
- Patterned fabric scraps
- Lace ribbon or trim
- Poly-fil stuffing
- Sewing machine
- Needle and thread
- Dressmaker pins

Instructions

STEP 1: Enlarge the fox body template to yield an 8 x 12$\frac{1}{2}$-inch pattern for fabric. Cut out the front and back pieces of the fox from solid-print fabric.

STEP 2: Cut out a 3$\frac{1}{2}$ x 2-inch-wide piece of white felt using the fox head template.

STEP 3: Cut out a circle shape for a nose from black felt.

STEP 4: Cut out a 4 x 5-inch heart shape from patterned fabric for the belly. Trim edges with pinking shears.

STEP 5: Cut 1 strip of lace ribbon or trim the width of the fox's front plus 1 inch, and cut another strip of lace for the fox's back ($\frac{1}{2}$ inch will be tucked in on each side when sewn).

STEP 6: Sew the white felt for the head to the front piece of the fox.

STEP 7: Use an embroidery needle and black embroidery thread to sew on the eyes and nose as shown.

STEP 8: Sew on a strip of lace ribbon or trim around the neck area of the front fox piece. Make sure to leave $1/2$ inch unsewn and overhanging the edges.

STEP 9: Sew the heart to the front of the fox.

STEP 10: Line up the front and back fox pieces to see where to sew the second strip of lace trim to the back piece of the fox. Sew the lace to the fox, making sure to leave $1/2$ inch unsewn and overhanging the edges.

STEP 11: Use the tail template to yield a tail size pattern of $9^{1}/_4$ x $3^{3}/_4$ inches. Cut the

tail shape from patterned fabric and sew it to the back of the fox, over the top of the lace trim.

STEP 12: Place the front and back pieces of the fox together, right sides facing each other. Pin to secure. Sew around the edges with a $1/4$-inch inseam. Leave an opening at the bottom.

STEP 13: Carefully turn the fox right side out and fill it with poly-fil stuffing.

STEP 14: Sew the gap closed with a blind stitch.

COLD HAM *and* COLD CHICKEN

Cold cuts of meat can be both fancy and satisfying. Buy a spiral-cut ham and a rotisserie chicken to make a simple basis for this dinner and then build around it. A menu featuring cold meat works well for a late-night meal, or for a very busy day when you don't have much time for cooking. All the recipes for Dinner at the Great House can be made ahead.

FRUIT
Pyramid

Some recipes for fruit pyramids suggest making a sugar paste to help hold the fruit together, but it can work equally well by using toothpicks or short bamboo skewers to keep the fruit in place.

Fruits that work well include apples, oranges, plums, pomegranates, pears, lemons, clementines, grapes, and cherries. You can also use fresh greenery to help decorate the fruit pyramid.

Select a large serving plate or stand. Place fruits for the base layer on the bottom in a triangle shape. Use larger fruits, such as oranges or apples, for the base layer. Hold the fruits together with toothpicks or skewers.

Pierce the tops of the pieces of fruit with toothpicks or skewers and slide another layer of fruit onto the first, making the next layer slightly smaller and closer to the center than the last. Continue this process with increasingly smaller layers until you have reached the top of your pyramid.

Fill in the gaps between the larger pieces of fruit with smaller fruit, such as grapes or cherries. Greenery also works well to fill in these spaces.

A fruit pyramid is a great way to show off your skills as a designer. Arrange the shapes and colors to make a stunning centerpiece. Design an all-citrus pyramid, for example, or a pyramid made only of pomegranates and yellow cherries. Choose fruit in season.

Fruit pyramids can make gorgeous centerpieces. Think of that dinner scene in the 1996 movie *Emma* with Gwyneth Paltrow.

KEY TO MY HEART
Children's APRON

Let kids in on Austen-inspired fun with this whimsical apron. Though the directions below are not suited for beginner sewers, they can still help with cutting and pinning. For a simplified version that beginner sewers can try, use pinking shears to cut out all fabric pieces so no hemming is needed.

Materials

1 (9$\frac{1}{2}$ x 5-inch) piece linen fabric

1 (16$\frac{1}{2}$ x 18$\frac{1}{2}$-inch) piece linen fabric

Dressmaker pins

Sewing machine

1 (32$\frac{1}{2}$ x 5$\frac{1}{2}$-inch) piece patterned fabric for the bottom ruffle

1 (9-inch-long) piece white ruffle trim for the top of apron

2 (18-inch) pieces white grosgrain ribbon for the neck ties

1 (68-inch-long) piece white grosgrain ribbon for the empire waist

1 (16-inch) piece decorative flower lace for the empire waist

1 (2 x 3-inch) piece white lace fabric

1 (4$\frac{1}{4}$ x 5$\frac{1}{4}$-inch) piece burlap

Skeleton key

Variety of white buttons (23 are used on the apron in the photo)

Embroidery needle and thread (blue and green is used in the apron shown)

Instructions

FOR THE APRON

STEP 1: Hem the edges of each piece of linen fabric using $\frac{1}{4}$-inch seam.

STEP 2: Center and pin the long edge of the smaller linen square to the shorter middle edge of the larger linen square. Using a zigzag stitch, sew the smaller linen square edge to the larger linen square edge.

STEP 3: Hem the edges of the bottom ruffle fabric using a $\frac{1}{4}$-inch seam. Using needle and thread, gather and overlap the fabric so it forms a long ruffle. Knot thread to secure the gathers.

STEP 4: Sew the bottom ruffle to the bottom of the apron using a running stitch.

STEP 5: Sew 9-inch-long white ruffle trim to the top of the apron.

STEP 6: Sew each piece of 18-inch-long grosgrain ribbon to the top of each side of the apron.

STEP 2: Place skeleton key in the middle of lace fabric as shown in photo. Place a smaller strip of the lace fabric over the "neck" of the key and hand-sew in place.

STEP 3: Using embroidery needle and thread, sew white buttons around the edge of the lace fabric. Alternate thread colors on the buttons.

STEP 7: Center decorative flower lace on top of the 68-inch-long grosgrain ribbon. Pin to empire waist of apron, making sure to cover any zigzag stitching with the decorative lace and ribbon. Sew all in place.

FOR THE BURLAP KEY RECTANGLE

STEP 1: Sew 2 x 3-inch piece white lace fabric to the center of the burlap rectangle.

STEP 4: Hand-sew the burlap key rectangle in place with a running stitch. Use a thread color to match the burlap so the stitches are not noticeable.

ASSORTMENT *of* CHEESES

Fancy cheeses are a great way to dress up your meal. You can have just a few or add more selections. Some great cheeses to try are Munster, Havarti, Swiss, Brie, Roquefort, Camembert, Chevre, Gouda, and Manchego. Slice beforehand or serve on a cheese board with a cheese knife for guests to slice their own.

Many entertaining menus and period cookbooks from Jane Austen's time list cold cuts of meat and poultry as well as an assortment of cheeses and fruit as different courses for dinner.

"Perfect for a house which had such a character of hospitality and ancient dignity to support."
—*Persuasion*

LOVELY
Burlap and Lace
WREATH

Materials

1 (12-inch) Styrofoam wreath form

2 (30-foot x 6-inch) rolls burlap garland (how much you use depends on how much the fabric is bunched) plus extra burlap for wrapping wreath form

Florist greening pins

2 yards lace ribbon

1 (1.75-pound) package white oven-bake clay (Sculpey)

Love stencil from page 140

Craft knife

Acrylic paint, color of choice

Scalloped circle paper punches, sizes $3^1/2$ inches and 2 inches

Book pages

3 brads

Ink in tea stain color

Paintbrush

Hot glue gun and glue sticks

Instructions

FOR THE WREATH

STEP 1: Wrap wreath form with burlap garland. Secure with florist greening pins.

STEP 2: Unroll the two burlap rolls. Take the two strips of burlap and fold each in half long ways. Position each strip so the edges face each other and are slightly overlapping. Pin in place. Sew overlapped edges, creating one strip of burlap that is like a long tube that's sewn down the middle.

STEP 3: Use a greening pin to secure one end of the burlap tube to the wreath form.

STEP 4: Start working around the wreath form, bunching the burlap garland and securing with greening pins as you go. Bunching the garland should result in poufs of material on the front of the wreath form.

STEP 5: Place the lace ribbon on top of the burlap poufs, tucking it in between the burlap folds. Secure with greening pins.

FOR THE CERAMIC "LOVE"

STEP 1: For the ceramic "love" shown in the photo, about half the package of oven-bake clay was used. Knead the clay until it's soft and smooth. Use a rolling pin to roll out the clay to 1/4-inch thickness on a cutting board.

STEP 2: Lay the "love" stencil on top of the clay and carefully cut out the letters using a craft knife.

STEP 3: Bake the clay "love" in the oven according to package directions (Sculpey brand takes 15 minutes at 275 degrees F). After baking, let ceramic cool for about an hour.

STEP 4: Paint "love" ceramic with desired acrylic paint color. Let dry.

STEP 5: Hang the ceramic from the wreath front with twine or hot glue it in place.

FOR THE FLOWERS

STEP 1: Using the larger scalloped paper punch, cut out 10 circles from book pages. Using the smaller scalloped paper punch, cut out 20 circles.

STEP 2: Make a stack of the large circles. Make 2 stacks of the smaller circles (10 circles in each stack). Use the end of a sharp pair of scissors to poke a hole through the center of each stack.

STEP 3: Poke a brad through the center of each paper stack and fold out brad ends to secure.

STEP 4: Using your fingers, start bunching up the top paper circle of the large stack and work your way down. Work the paper until you have a flower shape you like. Repeat this step for the smaller stacks.

STEP 5: Apply ink color to the edges of the paper layers using a paintbrush.

STEP 6: Attach flowers in place using hot glue and a glue gun.

PICKLED
Cucumbers

1$\frac{1}{2}$ cups water
$\frac{1}{2}$ cup white vinegar
1 teaspoon salt
$\frac{1}{2}$ teaspoon black pepper
1 English cucumber, peeled and thinly sliced
1 small red onion, peeled and thinly sliced

In a medium glass bowl, combine water and vinegar. Whisk in salt and pepper.
Add cucumber and onion slices and swirl. Taste for salt and adjust.
Add more vinegar or water to taste. Chill before serving.

Makes 4 servings

"Tell your father, with aunt Cass's love and mine, that the pickled
cucumbers are extremely good." —Letter from Jane Austen to her
nephew Edward, December 16, 1816

Jane Austen's mother, Cassandra, contributed a recipe for bread pudding to Martha Lloyd's collection of recipes in 1808. Charmingly, it was written out in rhyme. This recipe is not much different from Mrs. Austen's—bread, fruit (here apples rather than currants), spices, sugar, butter, milk, and eggs as a binder.

PUDDING

4 cups torn cinnamon-raisin bread pieces
2 cups peeled and sliced apples
1 cup brown sugar
$1^3/_4$ cups milk
$^1/_4$ cup butter
$^1/_2$ teaspoon vanilla extract
2 eggs

VANILLA SAUCE
$^1/_4$ cup sugar
$^1/_4$ cup brown sugar
$1^1/_2$ teaspoons cornstarch
$^1/_2$ cup milk
$^1/_2$ cup butter
1 teaspoon vanilla extract

Preheat oven to 350 degrees F. Spray a 7 x 11-inch baking dish with nonstick cooking spray.

In a large bowl combine the bread and apples. In a small saucepan over medium heat, combine the brown sugar, milk, and butter. Cook until butter is melted. Pour over bread mixture in bowl and toss.

In a small bowl, whisk together vanilla and eggs. Pour bread mixture into prepared dish and pour egg mixture over the top.

Bake for 40–50 minutes or until center is set and apples are tender.

While pudding is baking, prepare vanilla sauce by mixing together sugar and brown sugar in a medium saucepan. Stir cornstarch into milk and add to sugars along with butter. Bring to a boil, stirring frequently. Remove from heat and stir in vanilla.

Serve bread pudding topped with vanilla sauce.

Serves 8

CHAPTER 4

Emma

"Strawberries, and only
strawberries, could now be
thought or spoken of."
—*Emma*

*Emma's
Picnic*

MENU

Cucumber Sandwiches

Chicken Salad Sandwiches

Egg Sandwiches

Cold Asparagus

Strawberries

Cheesecake

CRAFTS

Emma and Mr. Knightley's
Paper Chandelier

Emma Paper Dolls

"Fancy That" Sandwich
Wrappers

Box Hill Picnic Plates

Perfect Picnic Suitcase

This chandelier would be wonderful hanging from the library ceiling at Hartfield. Just picture Emma sitting below it, plotting her next match! Note: Setting up the macramé hoops for hanging ahead of time will ensure the pinwheels don't get crushed.

EMMA AND MR. KNIGHTLEY'S *Paper* CHANDELIER

Materials

2 ($^3/_{16}$ x 27-inch-long) pieces white ribbon

1 (14-inch) macramé hoop

4 (16-inch-long) pieces monofilament illusion cord, transparent (clear-colored fishing line will also work)

100 ($6^1/_4$ x $9^1/_4$-inch) paperback pages for large pinwheels

1 (12-inch) macramé hoop

45 ($6^1/_4$ x $9^1/_4$-inch) paperback pages for small pinwheels

Double-sided cello tape, permanent

Regular cello tape

4 ($9^1/_2$-inch-long) "crystal" jewelry strings

4 (6-inch-long) "crystal" jewelry strings

Instructions

TO HANG THE HOOPS

 STEP 1: Tie one end of a piece of ribbon to the larger macramé hoop. Tie the other end of the ribbon to the opposite side of the hoop. Tie an end of the second piece of ribbon to the hoop halfway between where the first ribbon ends were tied. Tie the other end of the second piece of ribbon halfway between where the other end of the first ribbon ends were tied. The two ribbons should be squarely crisscrossed.

 STEP 2: Cut a small piece of ribbon and tie it around the ribbon pieces at their overlapping point. Tie another knot in the end of the small ribbon piece, creating a little loop. This is what will be placed on a hook so the chandelier can hang.

STEP 3: Tie one end of each illusion cord piece to the larger macramé hoop, making sure to space evenly between the ribbon ties. Tie the opposite end of each illusion cord piece to the smaller macramé hoop, making sure each cord will hang straight.

 STEP 4: Find a lower spot to hang the chandelier while you build and add the pinwheels. Then, when all the pinwheels are on the hoops, hang the chandelier from a hook on the ceiling.

 STEP 5: When the chandelier is hanging from the ceiling, tie the 8 "crystal" jewelry strings (long-short-long-short pattern) to the lower hoop, making sure to space the strings evenly around the hoop.

FOR THE LARGE PINWHEELS ON THE LARGE HOOP

 STEP 1: Each pinwheel will use 4 paper-back pages. Accordion fold each page widthwise with each fold being approximately 1 inch wide.

 STEP 2: When finished folding a page, fold it in half, creating a "fan."

 STEP 3: Use double-sided tape on the inside edge of the folded paper so the "fan" stays together.

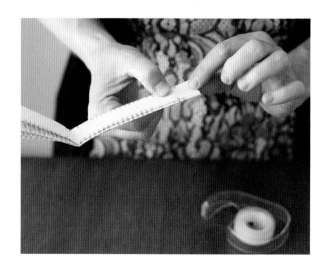

FOR THE SMALL PINWHEELS ON THE SMALL HOOP

🐚 **STEP 1:** Each pinwheel will use $1^1/_2$ paperback pages. Cut 45 paperback pages in half.

🐚 **STEP 2:** Accordion fold each half page widthwise, with each fold being approximately $^3/_4$ inch wide.

🐚 **STEP 3:** When finished folding a page, fold it in half, creating a "fan."

🐚 **STEP 4:** After 3 "fans" are made, attach them all with double-sided tape on the inside edges. To make the pinwheels more secure, use regular cello tape on the upper and lower edges of the "fans."

🐚 **STEP 4:** After 4 "fans" are made, attach them all with double-sided tape on the inside edges. To make the pinwheels more secure, use regular cello tape on the upper and lower edges of the "fans."

🐚 **STEP 5:** Before securing the last two fans of a pinwheel together, place it around the larger macramé hoop.

🐚 **STEP 6:** Repeat steps 1–5 to make 24 more pinwheels for the 14-inch hoop.

🐚 **STEP 5:** Before securing the last two fans of a pinwheel together, place it around the smaller macramé hoop.

🐚 **STEP 6:** Repeat steps 2–5 to make 29 more pinwheels for the 12-inch hoop.

The instructions here will make 2 Emma doll shapes. Make more dolls and then glue end to end to make a longer doll chain. This is a fun and creative activity for kids. Try your hand at drawing a top-hatted Mr. Knightley outline for kids to decorate.

EMMA
Paper
DOLLS

Materials

Emma Paper Doll template (page 142)

Craft knife, scissors, paper punches

1 (12 x 12-inch) piece kraft paper

Pencil

Variety of colored and patterned paper, book pages, ribbon and trimmings

Double-sided cello tape and craft glue

Instructions

 STEP 1: Copy the Emma template on page 142. Cut it out.

 STEP 2: Accordion fold the kraft paper so there are 2 folds in the paper. Place the doll pattern on a folded edge, with the skirt edge and hand end on a folded edge.

 STEP 3: Draw the outline of the doll onto the kraft paper and then cut it out. Unfold the paper to see two paper dolls. Lay them flat.

 STEP 4: Cut out dress shapes from colored and patterned paper and attach them to dolls using double-sided tape or craft glue. Add a Regency look by attaching a ribbon or strips of paper to create an empire waist on the dress. Add hair cutouts and other decorations as desired.

Use pretty patterned papers to wrap around the picnic sandwiches for Emma's Picnic Menu (see pages 80–82). Use scissors and paper punches to add a decorative touch, turning regular sandwiches into party pleasers.

"FANCY THAT"
Sandwich
WRAPPERS

Materials

Regular scissors

Variety of patterned papers (scrapbooking, giftwrap)

Scissors with decorative edges such as scallops and triangles

Paper punches in multiple designs

Instructions

 STEP 1: Cut strips of papers according to sandwich width sizes.

 STEP 2: Use decorative edge scissors and paper punches to create designs along the edges of the paper strips as desired.

 STEP 3: Wrap one paper strip around each sandwich to gauge paper over-lap. Make a small cut on the left side of one end, perpendicular to the edge. Make another small cut in the opposite end, perpendicular to the edge, but make the cut on the right side of the end. Wrap the strip around the sandwich and secure in place by interlocking the two small cuts you made.

CUCUMBER
Sandwiches

4 slices pumpernickel bread
1 container (8 ounces) spreadable cream cheese
1 English cucumber, peeled and sliced
Salt and pepper, to taste
Fresh dill for garnish

Spread each slice of bread with cream cheese. Arrange cucumber slices on top. Sprinkle with salt and pepper and garnish with sprigs of dill.

Makes 4 open-face sandwiches

Pretty sandwiches make for a pretty picnic or party.

CHICKEN SALAD
Sandwiches

4 rolls or croissants
2 cups shredded or cubed cooked chicken*
$\frac{1}{2}$ cup mayonnaise
$\frac{1}{2}$ cup plain yogurt
$\frac{1}{2}$ cup sliced celery
1 (8-ounce) can pineapple tidbits, drained
$1\frac{1}{2}$ cups halved seedless red grapes
$\frac{1}{2}$ cup slivered almonds, toasted

Gently mix together all ingredients for salad except almonds. Cover and refrigerate for at least 30 minutes. Before serving, stir in almonds and pile salad onto rolls or croissants.

*Rotisserie chicken works well.

Makes 4 sandwiches

EGG
Sandwiches

8 hard-boiled eggs, peeled and diced fine
1 cup mayonnaise
1 teaspoon mustard powder
Salt and pepper, to taste
8 slices white bread, crusts removed

In a medium bowl, gently mix eggs, mayonnaise, and mustard powder. Season with salt and pepper. Spread mixture evenly over 4 slices of bread and top with remaining 4 slices. Slice sandwiches in thirds.

Makes 12 small finger sandwiches

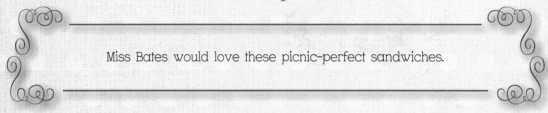

Miss Bates would love these picnic-perfect sandwiches.

COLD ASPARAGUS

2 pounds fresh asparagus, trimmed
$\frac{1}{4}$ cup white wine vinegar
2 teaspoons Dijon mustard
$\frac{1}{2}$ teaspoon ground ginger
$\frac{1}{4}$ teaspoon salt
$\frac{1}{2}$ teaspoon pepper
$\frac{1}{2}$ cup vegetable oil

Blanch asparagus by placing in boiling water until fork-tender but still crisp. Remove and plunge into ice water for about 30 seconds. Drain and chill in refrigerator.

In a small bowl combine the vinegar, mustard, ginger, salt, and pepper. Whisk in oil.

When ready to serve, arrange asparagus on a platter and drizzle with dressing.

Makes 8 servings

"There was a delicate fricassee of sweetbread and some asparagus brought in at first, and good Mr. Woodhouse, not thinking the asparagus quite boiled enough, sent it all out again."
—*Emma*

BOX HILL
Picnic
PLATES

> "It's such a happiness when good people get together." —*Emma*

Materials

Small artificial flowers that can be pressed flat (I used 4 flowers per plate)

4 (8-inch diameter) glass plates

2 (18 x 48-inch) moss mats (Instant Green brand found at Jo-Ann Fabric and Craft Store)

Scissors

Mod Podge, matte

Sponge brush

Bowl

Instructions

STEP 1: Remove flowers from stems and set aside.

STEP 2: Lay a glass plate front side down on a table. Lay a moss mat over the back of the plate and cut around the edges with scissors.

STEP 3: Remove the moss mat from the plate and lay it flat on the table. Place some flowers on the moss mat.

STEP 4: Apply a generous amount of Mod Podge to the back of the plate. Apply some Mod Podge to the flowers on the mat.

STEP 5: Carefully lift the plate by its edges and flip it over and lay it on top of the moss mat. Press down around the edges with your fingers.

STEP 6: Flip over the plate again so the front side is facing down. Lay it on top of an upside down bowl to dry for 48 hours. Every once in a while during the first 2–3 hours of drying, use your fingers to press the moss mat to the glass plate to ensure a tight bond.

STEP 7: Repeat steps 1–6 for the remaining plates.

TIP: Do not submerge the plates in soap and water to wash them. The moss mat and sealer are not waterproof. Instead, carefully wash the plate fronts with a little soap and water on a dishcloth.

STRAWBERRIES

2 pints fresh strawberries
Whipped cream

Serve a bowl of bright, freshly washed strawberries with stems intact.
Alternately you can remove stems and slice the strawberries,
sprinkle with a little white sugar and allow to macerate.

Serve in bowls with freshly whipped cream.

Enjoy your own Box Hill picnic with the recipes in this chapter, or
organize a strawberry-gathering party with friends!

Delicious food, good manners and a Perfect Picnic Suitcase are all that's needed for an outdoor gathering with friends.

PERFECT
Picnic SUITCASE

Materials

FOR THE SUITCASE EXTERIOR

1 suitcase with hard exterior (the one shown is 26 x 16 x 7$\frac{1}{2}$ inches)

Scissors

2 yards patterned fabric

Several fat quarters and fabric scraps in matching and coordinating patterns and colors

Tape measure

Mod Podge, matte

Sponge brush

FOR THE SUITCASE INTERIOR

Scissors

2 yards fabric to match exterior fabric

Hot glue gun and glue sticks

Ribbon for inside edge, wider style is better (I used 3 yards and 7 inches of ribbon for the suitcase shown)

4 (12-inch-long) pieces fabric ribbon to hold picnic plates

16 inches hook-and-loop Velcro, cut in 8 (2-inch) pieces (to hold the plates)

12 (4$\frac{1}{2}$-inch-long) pieces fabric ribbon to hold silverware, straws, or napkins

24 inches hook-and-loop Velcro, cut in 12 (2-inch) pieces (to hold silverware, straws, or napkins)

Instructions

FOR THE SUITCASE EXTERIOR

 STEP 1: Measure all sides of the suitcase exterior. Cut fabric to fit. To make it a little easier, cut smaller pieces of fabric rather than large single pieces. Note that I used a busier fabric pattern for the exterior, which helps to hide any cut edges.

 STEP 2: Using a sponge brush, apply Mod Podge to the front and back of fabric pieces and adhere to suitcase exterior, making sure to press out air bubbles where necessary. Let the Mod Podge dry for 24–48 hours before crafting the suitcase interior.

FOR THE SUITCASE INTERIOR

 STEP 1: Measure all sides of the suitcase interior. Cut fabric to fit each section. I was able to cover the interior of this suitcase using 5 pieces of the fabric for the different sections. Look at how the inside of your suitcase is constructed to determine the best way to cut fabric in order for it to fit correctly.

 STEP 2: Attach the fabric to the inside of the suitcase using hot glue. Work in small sections and apply small beads of glue rather than large blobs, which will show through the fabric and create a bumpy surface.

STEP 3: Adhere ribbon along the inside edge of the suitcase with hot glue, covering any raw edges of fabric that are showing.

 STEP 4: Measure where to place the fabric ribbon "crosses" to hold the plates.

Use hot glue to attach 8 (2-inch) pieces of the loop side of the Velcro to the inside of the suitcase lid.

 STEP 5: Glue the matching 8 (2-inch) pieces of the hook side of the Velcro to each end of the 4 (12-inch-long) pieces of fabric

 ribbon. Press the Velcro ends together to make the "crosses" that will hold the plates.

 STEP 6: For our suitcase, I made 12 ribbon loops to hold various picnic items. You may be able to use more or fewer ribbon loops, depending on your suitcase size. For stability, I used two ribbon loops to hold the ends of items at the same level (e.g., see lower-right photo of ribbon loops holding silverware on page 90).

STEP 7: Glue loop side of the Velcro to the end of a fabric ribbon piece, on the inside. Glue the hook side of the Velcro to the opposite end of the fabric ribbon piece, on the inside. Adhere one end of fabric ribbon to the suitcase fabric. The fabric ribbon loop that "matches" the loop you just made should be made and then glued so there's a 2-inch space between the two finished fabric loops. Repeat this step for however many fabric loops you would like to make.

Cheesecake

CRUST

1$\frac{1}{2}$ (8-ounce) bags ginger snap cookies, ground to fine crumbs
6 tablespoons butter, melted
1$\frac{1}{2}$ teaspoons minced orange zest

FILLING

1$\frac{1}{2}$ cups fresh orange juice
1 (3-inch) piece fresh ginger, thinly sliced
4 (8-ounce) packages cream cheese, room temperature
$\frac{2}{3}$ cup sugar
1 tablespoon minced orange zest
1 tablespoon vanilla extract
8 ounces Lindt white chocolate, melted
4 eggs

Preheat oven to 350 degrees F.

Stir together all ingredients for crust in a medium-sized bowl until crumbs are moist. Press into the bottom and up the sides of a 9- or 10-inch springform pan. Bake until done.

Boil the orange juice with the ginger in a small heavy saucepan until it is reduced to about 3 tablespoons.

In a large bowl, beat the cream cheese, sugar, orange zest, and vanilla together until smooth. Strain the reduced orange juice and add to the cream cheese mixture. Add the melted chocolate and beat until combined. Add eggs, one at a time, beating well after each addition.

Pour filling into the crust and bake until the top is dry and the sides are slightly puffy, about 50 minutes. The cheesecake should still jiggle when shaken. If the top cracks it is overdone. Transfer to a wire rack to cool. Cover and chill overnight in the refrigerator before serving.

Makes 12 servings

"At Devizes we had comfortable rooms and a good dinner, to which we sat down about five; amongst other things we had asparagus and a lobster, which made me wish for you, and some cheesecakes, on which the children made so delightful a supper as to endear the town of Devizes to them for a long time."
—Letter from Jane Austen to her sister Cassandra, May 17, 1799

A Rustic Dinner

MENU

French Pottage

Baked Apples

Homemade Butter

Oat Bread

Rustic Fruit Tart

CRAFTS

Cloth Book Jacket

Buttoned-Up Denim
and Lace Wristlet

Embellished Bookmark

Quilled Fringe Flowers
Serving Tray

Decorated Tart Stand

CHAPTER 5

Mansfield Park

*"A basin of soup would
be a much better thing
for you than tea."*
—*Mansfield Park*

Keep your Austen library collection pristine with cloth book jackets. Use coordinating fabrics for your jackets to have a matching collection for your bookshelf.

CLOTH
Book
JACKET

Materials

Hardcover book

Tape measure

Scissors

Fabric for outside, flaps, and inside of jacket

Dressmaker pins

Iron

Sewing machine

Cotton lace for book jacket spine

Gems and pearls

Needle and thread

Embroidery needle and thread in coordinating colors

Sequins

Instructions

STEP 1: Lay a hardcover book flat, spine side facing up.

STEP 2: Measure across the width of the book. Add $3/4$ inch to each end for hemming.

STEP 3: Measure the height of the book, adding $3/4$ inch to the top and bottom.

STEP 4: Cut out fabric for the outside of the jacket according to the measurements taken in steps 2 and 3. Wrap the fabric around the book, checking that the size is adequate.

STEP 5: Cut out fabric for the inside of the jacket, which should match the size of the fabric for the outside of the jacket.

STEP 6: Cut 2 pieces of fabric for the jacket flaps, sized at least 4 inches wide. The height should match the height of the outside and inside fabric pieces.

STEP 7: Lay each piece of flap fabric on top of the far ends of the outside fabric piece, right sides facing in. Pin in place and sew a $\frac{1}{4}$-inch seam with a running stitch.

STEP 8: Measure cotton lace to height of the book. Pin in place on top of the outside jacket fabric, over the spine area. Sew lace in place using a running stitch. Use needle and thread to hand-sew pearls and gems along the lace.

STEP 9: Use embroidery needle and thread to embellish any designs printed on the outside fabric piece. Add sequins if you like.

STEP 10: Lay the outside fabric on top of the inside fabric, right sides facing in. Pin in place. Leave about 5 inches of one flap end unpinned. Sew $\frac{1}{4}$-inch seam with a running stitch around all edges except the unpinned area. Pull right side of fabric through the unpinned area. Sew it closed with a blind stitch.

STEP 11: Wrap the cloth jacket around the outside of the book.

FRENCH
Pottage

2 (14-ounce) cans chicken broth
2–3 boneless, skinless chicken breasts
2 carrots, peeled and sliced
1 small yellow onion, peeled and quartered
¼ cup chopped fresh parsley
4–6 potatoes, peeled and quartered
Salt and pepper, to taste

Put all ingredients in a stockpot. Add water, if needed, to cover meat and vegetables by at least 2 inches. Cover, bring to a boil, and then reduce heat to low and simmer 1 hour.

Remove chicken. Mash vegetables with a potato masher, more or less, as desired depending on the consistency you would like for the soup. When chicken is cool enough to handle, cut into pieces and return to soup. Season with salt and pepper. Warm through before serving.

Makes 8 servings

The French word "pottage" originally meant a "standing" (heavy or thick) soup as opposed to a broth. A modern chicken soup is a nice rendering of the French pottage of Jane Austen's day. You can mash the vegetables to make the soup thicker or leave them chunky.

Echo the prim and proper style of Fanny Price with this respectable wristlet. A casual flair is added by using dark denim for the base, but a more formal look can be achieved with a thicker linen or twill.

BUTTONED-UP
Denim and Lace
WRISTLET

Materials

Pinking shears

1 (7 x 3-inch) piece patterned fabric

2 ($7\frac{1}{2}$ x $3\frac{1}{2}$-inch) pieces denim

1 (21 x $2\frac{1}{2}$-inch) piece tulle

Sewing needle

Thread

1 ($6\frac{3}{4}$ x $2\frac{1}{4}$-inch) piece ruffled eyelet lace

4 vintage-style buttons

1 ($34\frac{1}{2}$-inch) piece satin ribbon for tying

Dressmaker pins

2 (7-inch) pieces ruffled trimming

Instructions

STEP 1: Use pinking shears to trim the edges of the patterned fabric. Lay this fabric on the right side of one of the denim fabric pieces.

STEP 2: To prepare the tulle, start at one end and weave a needle with thread through the middle of the fabric, gathering and bunching it as you go. Knot the end of the thread to secure the bunched tulle. This piece should end up being 7 x 2½ inches in size. Place tulle on top of patterned fabric piece. Set aside the layered stack of denim, patterned fabric and tulle.

STEP 3: Weave a strip of satin ribbon through the eyelet holes of the ruffled lace. If your ruffled lace doesn't have holes, pin the ribbon to the top of the ruffled lace, in the middle.

STEP 4: Sew 4 vintage-style buttons, evenly spaced apart, to the top of the ribbon, attaching the piece of ruffled lace, the ribbon strip and the buttons together.

STEP 5: Lay the button-ribbon piece from step 4 on top of the fabric stack from step 2. Pin in place.

STEP 6: Sew a running stitch on both sides of the buttons, attaching all fabric layers together except for one of the denim pieces and the 2 pieces of ruffled trimming.

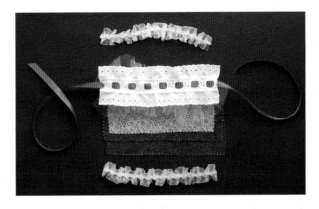

STEP 7: Face right sides of denim pieces together. Insert 1 piece of ruffled trimming along a long side of the denim.

STEP 8: Sew a running stitch along the edge, attaching the two denim pieces and ruffled trimming together.

STEP 9: Repeat steps 7 and 8 for the opposite side of the denim pieces.

STEP 10: Carefully turn the fabric "tube" right side out. Blind stitch the ends of the wristlet closed.

BAKED

Apples

6 apples
$\frac{1}{3}$ cup brown sugar
$\frac{1}{3}$ cup chopped nuts
$\frac{1}{3}$ cup raisins
$\frac{1}{4}$ cup oats
$\frac{1}{4}$ teaspoon cinnamon
$\frac{1}{8}$ teaspoon nutmeg
$\frac{1}{4}$ cup butter, softened
2 teaspoons lemon juice
1 cup apple juice

Preheat oven to 350 degrees F.

Core apples, being careful not to break through the bottoms. In a small bowl, mix brown sugar, nuts, raisins, oats, cinnamon, nutmeg, butter, and lemon juice. Using a spoon, fill each apple with some of the mixture.

Place apples in a shallow baking pan. Pour apple juice around apples and bake 40–45 minutes, or until apples are fork-tender. Serve warm with vanilla or cinnamon ice cream, or a dollop of whipped cream, if desired.

Makes 6 servings

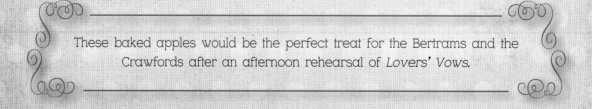

These baked apples would be the perfect treat for the Bertrams and the Crawfords after an afternoon rehearsal of *Lovers' Vows*.

> Making a bookmark is a must-have project in any book that has Jane Austen–inspired crafts. This one is easy to make and would be a lovely gift for any Janeite.

EMBELLISHED
Bookmark

Materials

- 6 inches black satin ribbon
- 1 ($6^1/4$ x $3^1/4$-inch) kraft paper tag
- 1 ($6^1/4$ x $3^1/4$-inch) piece decorative paper
- Paper punch with decorative edge design
- 1 (2 x $3^1/4$-inch) piece linen
- 1 (1 x 2-inch) piece linen for stamping
- 1 (2 x $3^1/4$-inch) piece cotton lace
- 1 (1 x $3^1/4$-inch) piece cotton lace
- Hot glue gun and glue sticks
- Decorative button
- Alphabet stamps
- 1 (3 x 4-inch) Easy-to-Cut Lino block
- Black waterproof ink sponge dauber
- Stapler

Instructions

STEP 1: Thread the ribbon through the hole in the top of the tag. Tie a knot.

STEP 2: Use the paper punch to make a decorative edge along the long sides of the decorative piece of paper.

STEP 3: Glue supplies to the top of the bookmark in this order:
- decorative piece of paper
- larger piece of linen
- larger piece of cotton lace
- decorative button

STEP 4: Glue the smaller piece of cotton lace to the bottom of the bookmark.

STEP 5: Stamp a book title on the smaller piece of linen and set aside.

FOR THE SILHOUETTE STAMP

 STEP 1: Copy and reduce the Jane silhouette template on page 138 to 70 percent. Cut it out and place it on top of a lino block. Use a pencil to trace an outline of the silhouette onto the block.

 STEP 2: Use a stamp-carving tool to cut away the negative space around the silhouette outline.

 STEP 3: Use a sponge dauber to apply black waterproof ink to the silhouette stamp. Stamp the design onto the decorative piece of paper. Embellish stamp as desired (I used pearl stickers on the neckline).

 STEP 4: Staple the smaller piece of linen with book title just below the silhouette stamp.

TIP: Make bookmarks that have all six Austen book titles to give as a gift set. These can also serve as take-home gifts for an Austen-themed party.

HOMEMADE
Butter

1 half pint heavy cream
$\frac{1}{4}$ teaspoon salt

Pour cream into a blender. Process for 10 minutes, or until the butter separates. Strain off the liquid and discard.

Put the butter in a colander and knead under cold running water for several minutes to work out any remaining buttermilk (otherwise the butter will spoil quickly).

Knead in salt. Roll into a log and wrap in waxed paper to store in the refrigerator.

Variation: Make herb butter by mixing in a couple teaspoons of chopped fresh herbs. Try dill butter, chive butter, or rosemary butter.

Makes $\frac{1}{2}$ cup butter

This butter can be made by shaking the cream in a clean Mason jar with a tight-fitting lid. Follow the instructions, except shake your cream for 15–20 minutes by hand.

OAT
Bread

2¼ cups boiling water
1¾ cups steel-cut oats
1 tablespoon salt
3 tablespoons butter
2 tablespoons brown sugar
2 packages dry yeast
½ cup warm water
3¼ cups flour, divided
3 cups whole wheat flour
Egg wash or melted butter

Combine boiling water, oats, salt, butter, and brown sugar in the bowl of a stand mixer and let stand for 25 minutes.

Dissolve yeast in warm water; let stand 5 minutes. Add to oat mixture.

Measure 2¾ cups flour and 3 cups whole wheat flour and gradually add to oat mixture. Beat on medium until well blended.

Turn out dough onto a floured board and knead until smooth and elastic, about 8 minutes. Add enough of the remaining flour, 1 tablespoon at a time, to prevent dough from sticking to your hands. Dough is rather sticky.

Place in a large bowl coated with nonstick cooking spray, turning to coat. Cover and let rise in a warm place for 1 hour or until doubled in size. Punch down, cover, and let rest 5 minutes. Divide in half. Shape into two rounds and brush tops with egg wash or melted butter. Sprinkle more oats on top.

Place on baking sheets that have been generously sprayed with nonstick cooking spray. Cover and let rise for 30 more minutes or until double in size.

Preheat oven to 350 degrees F. Bake for 45 minutes until loaves are browned on bottom and sound hollow when tapped. Remove from pan and cool on wire racks.

Makes 2 loaves

A perfect accompaniment to French Pottage.

QUILLED *Fringe Flowers* SERVING TRAY

Decorating objects with rolled papers was a popular pastime during the late eighteenth and early nineteenth centuries. Once you learn how to use the tool, it's surprisingly easy to design all kinds of flowers for your serving tray.

Materials

FOR THE SERVING TRAY

Green and gold acrylic paint (optional)

E6000 adhesive

2 C-shaped drawer handles (find at home-improvement or hardware stores)

11 x 14-inch frame matted to 8 x 10 inches (must have depth of $\frac{1}{2}$ inch so quilled flowers won't be smashed by the frame glass)

FOR THE FLOWERS

Quilling tool

$\frac{1}{8}$ x 12-inch quilling paper strips in a variety of colors

1 piece premium white cardstock

Scissors

Straight-edged paper cutter for cutting wider strips of paper

Variety of paper strips from books and colored papers, cut with paper cutter

Elmer's white glue

Cotton swabs

Instructions

FOR THE SERVING TRAY

 STEP 1: For a distressed effect, add green and gold paints to the frame.

 STEP 2: Use adhesive to attach drawer handles to the front of the frame. Set aside and let dry.

FOR THE FLOWERS

 STEP 1: Place the end of a $\frac{1}{8}$ x 12-inch strip of quilling paper in the slot of the quilling tool. Use your fingers to guide the paper as you turn the tool and wrap the paper onto the tool. Use a cotton swab to

apply glue to the end of the paper strip and adhere it to the wrapped-paper disk, which will become the center of a flower. Slide the flower center off the tool and apply glue over one side to secure.

 STEP 2: To create a fringe flower, use a wider paper strip. The wider the paper strip, the longer the fringe will be on a finished flower. Use scissors to make cuts along the edge of the paper strip, creating the fringe. Wrap the end of the paper strip around the quilling tool, as done in step 1. Secure the end and back of the fringed disk with glue and let dry. Use your fingers and the end of the quilling tool to fan out the fringe, creating an open-flower effect.

 STEP 3: Now that you understand how to build the flower centers and fringe, you can make flowers larger or smaller depending on how many strips of paper are glued together (end to end) and then rolled up on the tool. To create one complete flower, glue an end of a paper strip for the flower center to the end of a fringed paper strip (and glue on more fringe strips as desired for flower size). Roll up the long strip of papers and secure with glue.

 STEP 4: Once all the flowers are made, position them on the white cardstock as desired.

FOR THE LEAVES

 STEP 1: Roll green quilling paper around the quilling tool but instead of gluing the

end for a tight roll, slide the rolled paper off the tool and place it on a table to relax a little.

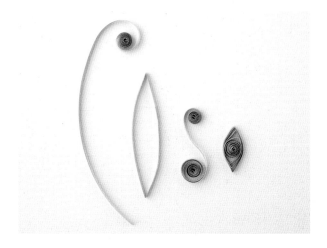

 STEP 2: Using your thumbs and forefingers, pinch the paper on one or both sides to form leaf shapes. Add glue to the end of the paper strip and glue it in place.

PUT IT TOGETHER

 STEP 1: Glue all the flowers and leaves to the white cardstock in a similar design as shown.

 STEP 2: Once the quilled floral design is complete and dry, place it inside the frame.

RUSTIC *Fruit* TART

CRUST
1¼ cups flour
2 tablespoons sugar
½ teaspoon salt
½ cup unsalted butter, chilled, cut into small pieces
3–4 tablespoons ice water

FRUIT FILLING
4 cups fresh sliced peaches
¼ cup sugar
1 pinch salt
1 teaspoon lemon or orange zest
3 tablespoons flour
½ teaspoon vanilla extract

To make the crust, combine flour, sugar, and salt in a large bowl. Add butter and work with a pastry blender or two knives until mixture resembles coarse meal. Add water, 1 tablespoon at a time. Mix until dough comes together. Add more water if needed.

Form the dough into a flat disc and wrap in plastic wrap. Chill for at least 1 hour before rolling.

In a large bowl toss together ingredients for the fruit filling; set aside.

Remove pastry disc from refrigerator and place on a floured surface or roll between 2 pieces of parchment paper. Roll to ⅛ inch thick. Place on a large baking sheet or pizza pan that has been prepared with nonstick cooking spray.

Spread filling in the center, leaving a couple of inches of dough around the edges. Fold the edges in 1–2 inches, and push down over the top of the fruit filling leaving the center exposed.

Bake for 45–50 minutes, or until crust is browned and fruit is hot and bubbling.

Makes 8 servings

A free-form tart, or galette, makes a nice finish to a rustic meal. Make this recipe in the late summer or early fall when fresh fruit is abundant. In addition to peaches, you can also try other fresh fruit such as blackberries, raspberries, apples, pears, or figs

> Elegance meets country rustic when this dessert stand is used to serve the Rustic Fruit Tart (see page 113) to dinner guests.

DECORATED *Tart* STAND

Materials

1 (12-ounce) can spray paint, glossy indoor/outdoor quality in color of choice

1 (12-inch-tall) plastic candlestick holder from craft store

Small plastic gems

1 (12-inch-diameter) round glass plate

Needle-nose tweezers

E6000 adhesive

Bowl

Stenciling paint dauber

Doily stencil (Martha Stewart)

Glass paint, gold

Instructions

STEP 1: Spray paint candlestick holder and let dry. Apply several thin coats for best coverage.

STEP 2: Apply the small plastic gems to the edge of the plate using needle-nose tweezers and E6000 adhesive. Let dry thoroughly. Applying the gems will take some time, but your patience will result in a fabulous dessert plate that can be used for more than a tart!

STEP 3: Place plate front side down on an upside down bowl. Use a dauber and doily stencil to paint a design on the back of the plate. Let the paint dry according to package directions.

STEP 4: Apply adhesive to the top rim of the candlestick holder. Pick up the plate and press the middle of it onto the top of the candlestick holder. Let it dry.

TIP: Do not submerge the tart stand in soap and water. It is not waterproof. Instead, use a little soap and water on a dishcloth to clean the plate of the stand.

CHAPTER 6

Pride and Prejudice

"You shall all have a bowl of
punch to make merry."
—*Pride and Prejudice*

Netherfield Ball

MENU

Regency Ball Negus

Poached Salmon

White Soup

Melon

Apricot Ice Cream

Lydia's Trifle

CRAFTS

I Heart Mr. Darcy Pillow

Stenciled Wine Glasses

I'd Rather Be Dancing T-Shirt

True Love Blanket

Charming Chimes

I HEART
Mr. Darcy
PILLOW

A decorative pillow such as this one offers the right amount of comfort when cozying up with a copy of *Pride and Prejudice*. Once you learn how easy it is to make the stencil, you'll be creating stencil designs to embellish almost anything in your home.

Materials

FOR THE PILLOW

1 (13$\frac{1}{2}$ x 19-inch) piece burlap

1 (13$\frac{1}{2}$ x 19-inch) piece white muslin for the lining

1 (13$\frac{1}{2}$ x 19-inch) piece blue ticking fabric (or other patterned fabric)

Scissors

Dressmaker pins

Matching all-purpose thread

Sewing machine

1 (12-ounce) bag poly-fil stuffing

Sewing needle

FOR THE STENCIL

I Heart Mr. Darcy template (see page 142)

1 (11-inch) roll adhesive stencil film

Craft knife

Self-healing cutting mat

Black permanent marker

Instructions

 STEP 1: Photocopy the I Heart Mr. Darcy template. Increase the size so it can fit on an 8$\frac{1}{2}$ x 11-inch piece of paper.

 STEP 2: Cut a piece of adhesive stencil film that's slightly larger than the template paper copy. Use painter's tape to secure each side of the template to the stencil film (as shown in photo). Lay the template and film on top of a cutting mat.

STEP 3: Use a craft knife to cut around the edges of each letter and the heart shape. Note that the centers of the "D" and "a" have no bridges connecting them to their letters, so take extra care in keeping track of these when you remove the letter cutouts. Remove the template copy to reveal the stencil.

 STEP 4: Iron the burlap so it's flat for stenciling. Remove the back layer of the adhesive stencil and lay the sticky side in the middle of the burlap fabric. Lay the sticky centers for the "D" and "a" in place.

 STEP 5: Follow the stencil and use a black permanent marker to color in the letters and heart.

 STEP 6: Arrange the burlap and ticking fabrics so the fronts are facing each other. Place the muslin fabric between the burlap and ticking fabrics. Since burlap has such a large weave, the muslin will be necessary in order to keep the poly-fil stuffing from peeking out between the burlap fibers. To secure the three pieces of fabric together, pin $1/2$ inch from the edge, all the way around. This will help to keep everything straight for sewing.

 STEP 7: Use a sewing machine to sew the fabrics together with a running stitch, leaving a $1/2$-inch seam allowance. Make sure to backstitch where you begin and end sewing so the thread doesn't unravel later. Leave a quarter to one-half of the bottom side of the pillow unsewn. This will be the opening for turning the fabric right side out before stuffing. If you didn't remove the pins as you sewed, check now to ensure that all pins are removed.

 STEP 8: To avoid fabric bulk in the corners, cut off each corner. Make sure you don't cut into the seam. Turn the fabric right side out.

 STEP 9: In the unsewn opening, create a pouch by separating the muslin fabric from the ticking fabric. Stuff the pillow with poly-fil stuffing. Use your hands to evenly distribute the filling to avoid lumps.

 STEP 10: Using a needle and thread, sew the opening closed with a blind stitch.

REGENCY *Ball* NEGUS

1 pint port wine*
1 lemon
$\frac{1}{4}$ pound sugar
Grated nutmeg to taste
1 quart boiling water

Place the wine in a nonmetallic heatproof serving pitcher or container. Zest the lemon in long strips and add to the sugar, then squeeze the lemon juice into the wine. Add the zest and sugar to the wine, along with a little nutmeg; pour the boiling water over all. Stir until the sugar dissolves. When the beverage has cooled a bit, remove the lemon zest strips and serve.

*For a tasty nonalcoholic version, substitute cranberry juice.

Makes 14 ($\frac{1}{2}$-cup) servings

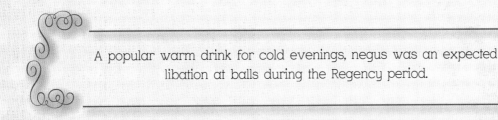

A popular warm drink for cold evenings, negus was an expected libation at balls during the Regency period.

Pamper yourself and a few guests with this set of wine glasses adorned with a golden design worthy of those in high society. Fill with Regency Ball Negus (see page "Regency Ball Negus" on page 121) and rejoice until dawn. Cheers!

STENCILED *Wine* GLASSES

Materials

4 wine glasses

Rubbing alcohol and cotton balls

Adhesive stencils (the ones used here are from Martha Stewart)

Small dauber

Metallic Opaque glass paint in Yellow Gold (Martha Stewart)

Instructions

 STEP 1: Clean outside of glasses with rubbing alcohol and cotton balls to remove any oils from handling.

 STEP 2: Place adhesive stencils on glasses where desired.

 STEP 3: Use a small dauber to apply glass paint over the top of the stencil. Tip: Put a small amount of paint on a paper plate and then dip the dauber in. Remove excess paint from the dauber by dabbing the dauber on the paper plate. Designs will be more successful if using a small amount of paint. Let paint dry.

 STEP 4: Peel stencils off glasses.

 STEP 5: Cure paint on glasses according to paint package directions.

I'd rather be dancing at the

Netherfield
Ball

Celebrate *Pride and Prejudice* by decorating the front of a t-shirt with this iron-on design. After all, who wouldn't rather be dancing at the Netherfield Ball?

I'd RATHER BE *Dancing* T-SHIRT

Materials

I'd Rather Be Dancing T-Shirt template (page 142)

1 (8$\frac{1}{2}$ x 11-inch) sheet image transfer paper for inkjet printer (I used Jolee's Easy Image brand)

White cotton t-shirt

Iron and ironing board

Needle and thread

2 strips fabric lace trim for edge of t-shirt sleeves (I used pieces sized approximately 17 inches long)

Instructions

 STEP 1: Copy the template so it's sized to fit an 8$\frac{1}{2}$ x 11-inch piece of paper. The template is backwards so it will be facing the right way once the design is transferred to the t-shirt and ironed in place.

 STEP 2: Using an inkjet printer, copy the template to the image transfer paper. Place the printed image face down on the t-shirt. Follow package directions to transfer the design to the t-shirt.

 STEP 3: Use needle and thread to hand-sew each strip of fabric lace to the outside edge of each sleeve.

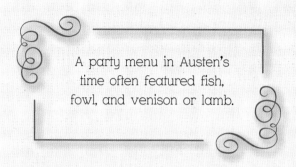

A party menu in Austen's time often featured fish, fowl, and venison or lamb.

POACHED
Salmon

1 fillet fresh salmon (2 to 3 pounds)
1 small onion
1 teaspoon olive oil
1 lemon
Fresh dill for garnish

Preheat oven to 325 degrees F. Place salmon in a poaching dish and fill the pan with $\frac{1}{2}$ inch of water. Bake 20 to 30 minutes. While the salmon is baking, thinly slice the onion and sauté it in olive oil. Cut the lemon in half; slice one half into thin slices.

When salmon is done, remove it from oven and transfer to a serving plate. Squeeze juice of the remaining lemon half over it. Garnish with lemon slices, sautéed onion, and dill.

Makes 8 to 12 servings

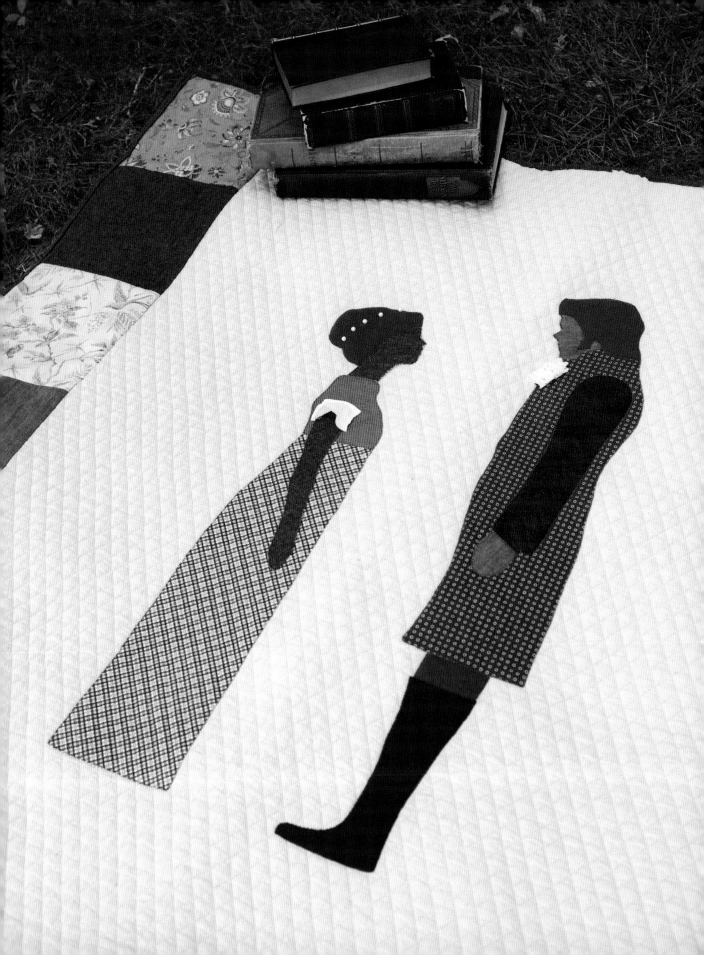

These silhouettes were inspired by the characters in the 2005 *Pride and Prejudice* film starring Keira Knightley and Matthew Macfayden.

TRUE *Love* BLANKET

Materials

Elizabeth and Darcy silhouette templates (see page 143)

Scissors

Variety of cotton and felt fabrics to use for appliqués

1 (40 x 70-inch) piece pre-quilted fabric for the front

Fusible web (I used Pellon brand Heat-N-Bond light)

Iron

2 (28 x 70-inch) pieces pre-quilted fabric for the back, sewn together with $\frac{1}{4}$-inch seam (finished size is 54 x 70 inches)

Tape measure

16 (10 x 10-inch) fabric squares in coordinating colors and patterns

Needle and thread

Dressmaker pins

Binding

Sewing machine

Instructions

FOR THE FRONT

 STEP 1: Enlarge the Elizabeth and Darcy silhouette templates by 380 percent. Cut out silhouette shapes from the cotton and felt fabrics as desired.

 STEP 2: Attach the appliqués to the front of the quilt using the fusible appliqué method. Follow package directions for the fusible web used. Repeat this step for all silhouette pieces.

 STEP 3: To secure appliqués even more, sew a zigzag stitch around all appliqué areas. I added lace and pearl embellishments to Elizabeth's hair and dress sleeve. I sewed a folded scrap of lace to the upper part of Darcy's jacket. Add any other embellishments as desired.

FOR THE BORDER

 STEP 1: For each side of the blanket front, pin edges of 8 (10 x 10-inch) fabric pieces together and sew a $\frac{1}{4}$-inch seam along each edge. When finished, there should be 2 strips of fabric squares sewn together (one for each side of the blanket front).

 STEP 2: Pin each strip of squares to the sides of the blanket front. Sew strips to the blanket with a $\frac{1}{4}$-inch seam.

PUT IT TOGETHER

 STEP 1: Lay the front piece of the blanket on top of the back piece of the blanket, wrong sides together. Pin to secure.

 STEP 2: Pin binding to the outside edges of the blanket.

 STEP 3: Sew around the blanket edge to attach all the layers together.

WHITE
Soup

1 chicken breast
2 quarts veal or chicken broth
2 ounces blanched almonds, ground very fine
1 egg yolk
¼ cup cream
Salt and pepper
Dash of lemon juice
Dash of cayenne pepper
2 ounces toasted almonds to garnish

In a large stockpot, simmer chicken breast in broth until cooked through. When meat is cool enough to handle, cut in small pieces and rub through a sieve into the broth. Push the ground almonds through the sieve into the soup.

Beat the egg yolk with the cream and add to the soup. Let sit for 1 to 2 hours. Reheat below boiling point. Do not overheat or egg will curdle. Season with salt, pepper, lemon juice, and cayenne.

Garnish with toasted almonds.

Serves 6

In *Pride and Prejudice*, Mr. Bingley famously announces that he cannot send out the invitations to the Netherfield Ball until he is sure Nicholls has prepared enough white soup. Although the classic recipe itself is somewhat bland, your guests will enjoy white soup for a more authentic Austen experience.

Materials

5 pieces vintage silverware

Drill with $\frac{1}{8}$-inch drill bit

Variety of costume gemstones

Jewelry pearls (with hole through center)

Needle-nose tweezers

E6000 adhesive

1 (6-yard) package 20-gauge wire, silver-plated

Wire cutters

Round bending pliers for wire

Strong stick or piece of driftwood

CHARMING
Chimes

These chimes have added character by using antique silverware and serving pieces, which are easily found at most secondhand stores. These would look wonderful in the garden of a country home or estate, or your backyard will do nicely too. Over time, the chimes will weather to a lovely patina.

Instructions

 STEP 1: Use clamps to hold silverware in place while drilling a hole in the top of each handle.

 STEP 2: While holding a gemstone with tweezers, place a drop or two of adhesive on the back. Carefully place gemstone on silverware. Continue until all pieces of silverware are decorated. Let dry overnight.

 STEP 3: Cut 5 pieces of wire: 3 pieces at about 11–12 inches long and 2 at about 8–9 inches long. It's better to have the wire a little longer since you can cut off any excess using the wire cutters.

 STEP 4: Thread wire through the hole in the handle of a piece of silverware.

 STEP 5: Add some jewelry pearls to the wire end and then use bending pliers to bend and twist the wire to secure. Repeat this step when attaching the tops of wires to a strong stick, but instead of threading the wire through a hole, wrap it around the stick, add pearls, and secure by bending and twisting the wire.

 STEP 6: Cut two pieces of wire 13–14 inches long. Use bending pliers to bend and twist each wire around the end of the stick. Twist wire into a loop at the top, which is used to hang the wind chimes.

APRICOT
Ice Cream

1 pint whipping cream
1 (6-ounce) can evaporated milk
Juice of $\frac{1}{2}$ lemon
Juice of $\frac{1}{2}$ orange
1 cup sugar
$1\frac{1}{2}$ cups sweetened apricot nectar

Mix all ingredients together in a large bowl or pitcher. Pour into a small ice cream maker and follow manufacturer's instructions.

Makes 2 quarts

Ice creams, ices, and frozen molded desserts in Jane Austen's day were made in a sabotiere, a device very similar to a modern-day ice cream maker. Ice cream was usually a treat of the wealthier class, who had large country estates, many of which had an ice house on the grounds. The ice houses were often dug into hillsides or were underground. Their stores were replenished with blocks of ice cut from rivers or lakes in winter.

LYDIA'S
Trifle

1 small box cook & serve vanilla pudding
1 angel food cake
½ cup raspberry jam
1 pint fresh berries
½ pint whipping cream
½ cup sliced almonds

Make pudding according to package directions. Set aside to cool. Cut cake into 1-inch cubes. Place in the bottom of a large glass bowl or a trifle serving dish. Drizzle with jam.

Pour pudding over the top of cake and jam. Scatter berries over the top. Whip and sweeten cream. Spread over the top of berries. Sprinkle with almonds before serving.

Makes 10 servings

A proper English trifle is made with real egg custard poured over sponge cake soaked in fruit and sherry and topped with whipped cream. This version is somewhat modernized.

Jane Silhouette Placemats

Enlarge to 150%

Emma

Northanger Abbey

Pride and Prejudice

Sense and Sensibility

Persuasion

Mansfield Park

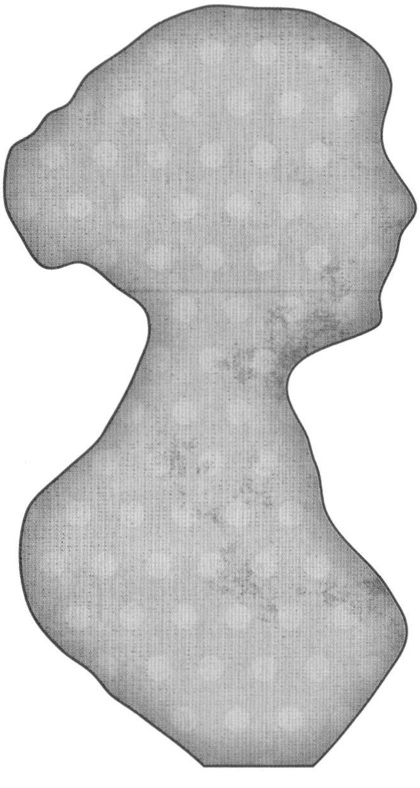

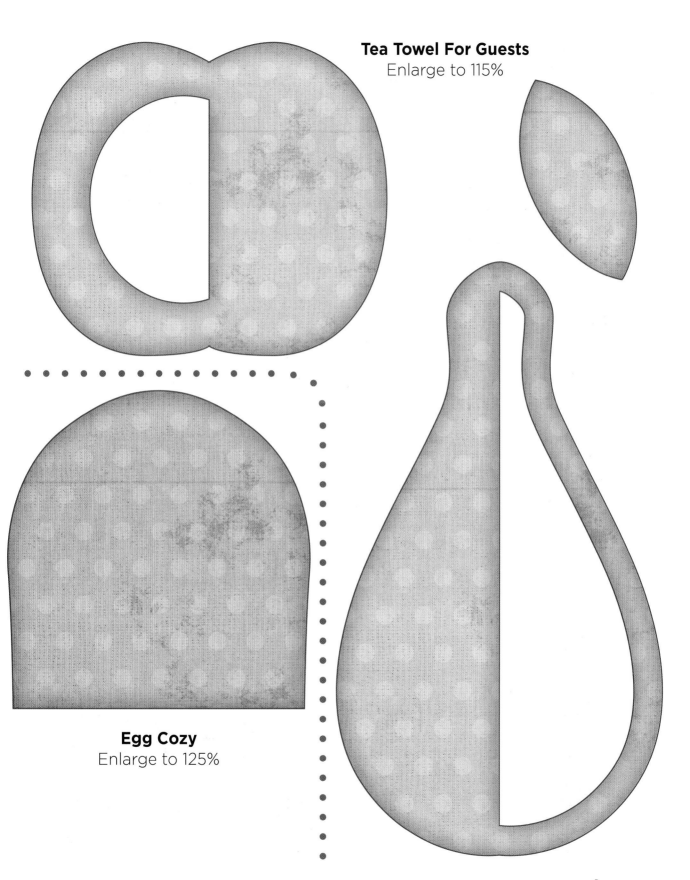

Tea Towel For Guests
Enlarge to 115%

Egg Cozy
Enlarge to 125%

Margaret's Vintage Fabric Garland

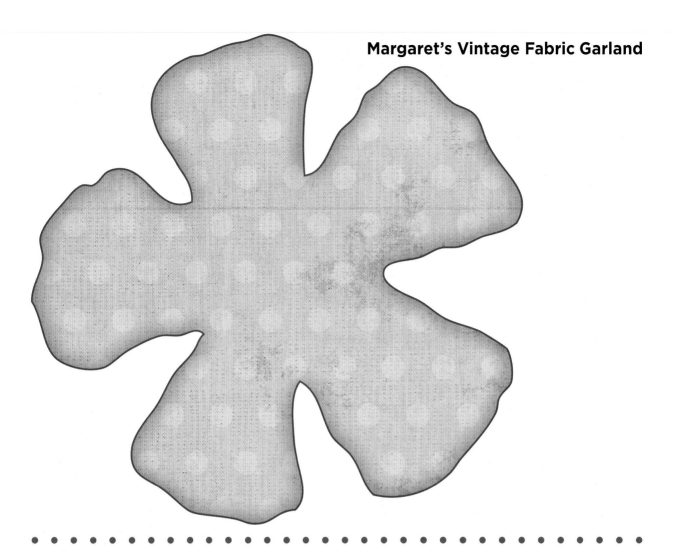

Lovely Burlap and Lace Wreath
Enlarge to 120%

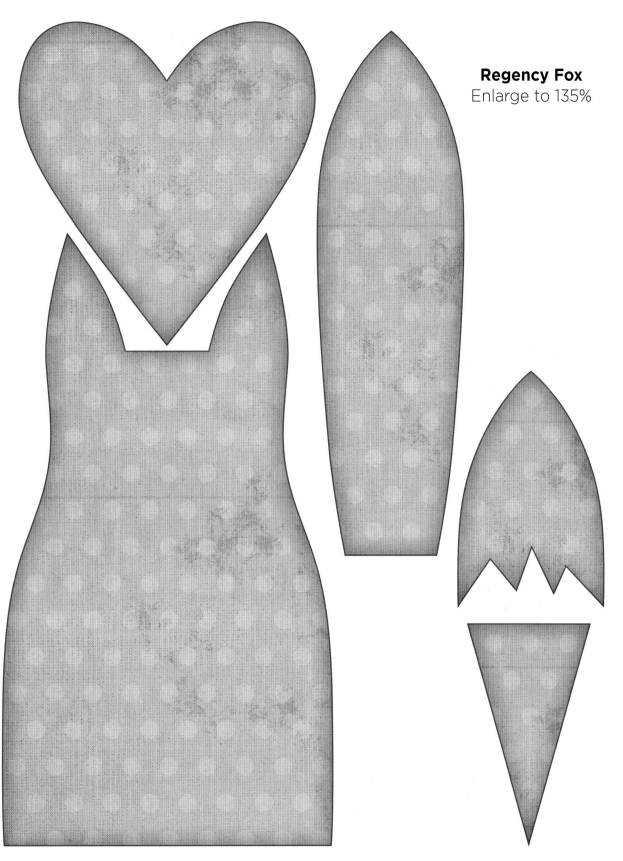

Regency Fox
Enlarge to 135%

I ♥ Mr. Darcy

I Heart Mr. Darcy Pillow
Enlarge to 150%

Emma Paper Dolls

I'd rather be dancing at the

Netherfield Ball

I'd Rather Be Dancing T-Shirt
Enlarge to 110%

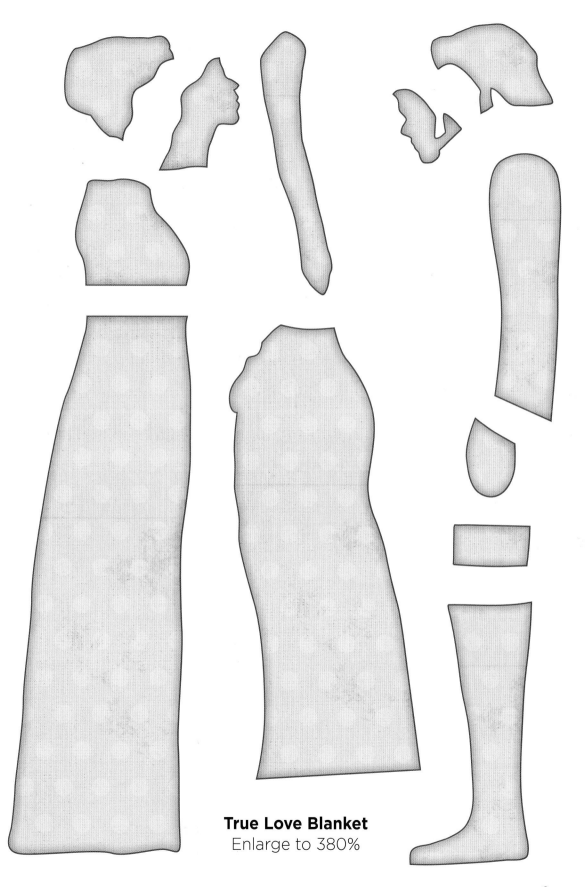

True Love Blanket
Enlarge to 380%

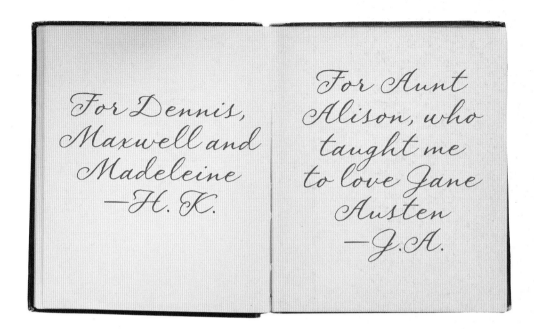

For Dennis, Maxwell and Madeleine
—H. K.

For Aunt Alison, who taught me to love Jane Austen
—J. A.

First Edition
18 17 16 · 15 14   5 4 3 2 1

Crafts © 2014 Hollie Keith
Recipes © 2014 Jennifer Adams
Photographs © 2014 Susan Barnson Hayward

All rights reserved. No part of this book may be reproduced by any means whatsoever without written permission from the publisher, except brief portions quoted for purpose of review.

Published by
Gibbs Smith
P.O. Box 667
Layton, Utah 84041

1.800.835.4993 orders
www.gibbs-smith.com

Designed by Cherie Hanson
Photography assistants:
Natalie Bernhisel-Robinson and Laura Hope Mason, prop stylists;
Camille Whitehead, food stylist
Printed and bound in China

Gibbs Smith books are printed on either recycled, 100% post-consumer waste, FSC-certified papers or on paper produced from sustainable PEFC-certified forest/controlled wood source. Learn more at www.pefc.org.

Library of Congress Cataloging-in-Publication Data

Keith, Hollie.
  So Jane : crafts and recipes for an Austen-inspired life / Hollie Keith ; recipes by Jennifer Adams ; photographs by Susan Barnson Hayward. — First edition.
      pages cm
  ISBN 978-1-4236-3323-5
1. Handicraft. 2. Cooking. 3. Cooking, English. 4. Austen, Jane 1775-1817—Miscellanea. 5. Austen, Jane, 1775-1817—Characters—Miscellanea. 6. Austen, Jane, 1775-1817—Settings—Miscellanea. I. Adams, Jennifer, 1970- II. Title.
  TT157.K395 2014
  745.5—dc23
                                                   2013031760